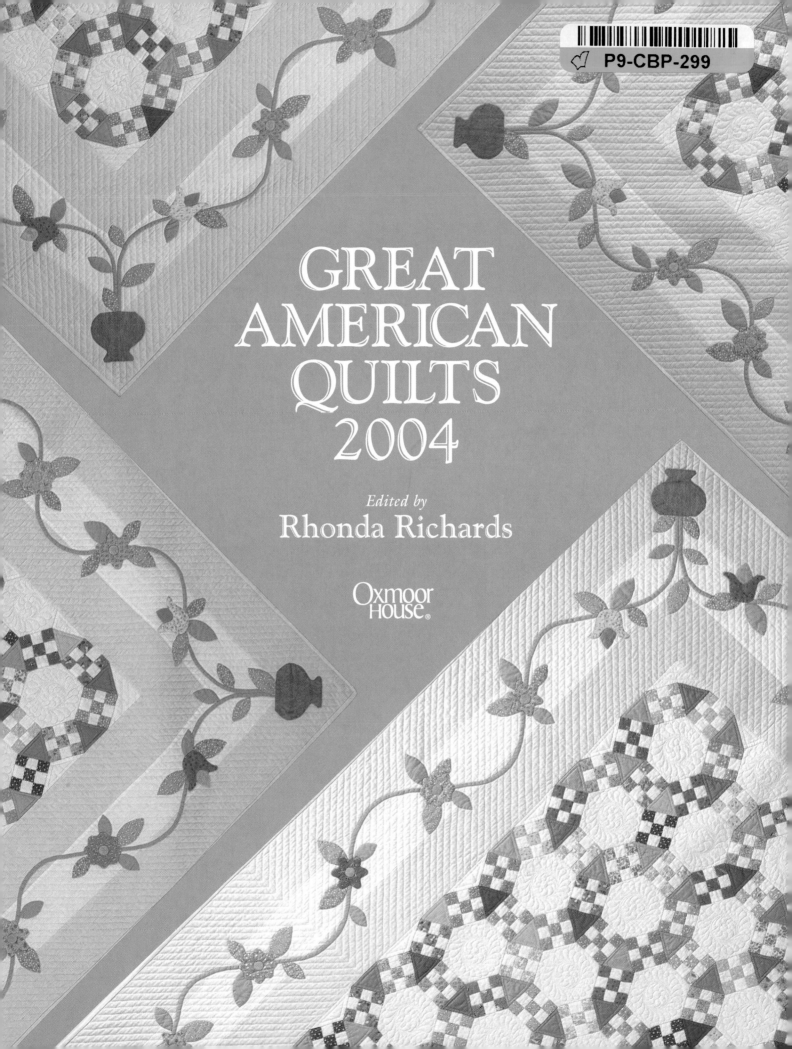

P9-CBP-299

GREAT AMERICAN QUILTS 2004

Edited by
Rhonda Richards

Oxmoor House®

Great American Quilts 2004

©2003 by Oxmoor House, Inc.
Book Division of Southern Progress Corporation
P.O. Box 2463, Birmingham, Alabama 35201

Published by Oxmoor House, Inc., and Leisure Arts, Inc.

All rights reserved. No part of this book may be reproduced in any form or by any means without the prior written permission of the publisher, excepting brief quotes in connection with reviews written specifically for inclusion in magazines or newspapers, or single copies strictly for personal use.

Hardcover ISBN: 0-8487-2630-8
Softcover ISBN: 0-8487-2645-6
Printed in the United States of America
First Printing 2003
To order additional publications, call 800-765-6400.

Editor-in-Chief: Nancy Fitzpatrick Wyatt
Executive Editor: Katherine M. Eakin
Art Director: Cynthia R. Cooper
Copy Chief: Allison Long Lowery
Editor: Rhonda Richards
Editorial Assistant: Dawn Russell
Designer/Illustrator: Kelly Davis
Senior Photographer: Jim Bathie

Senior Photo Stylist: Kay Clarke
Publishing Systems Administrator: Rick Tucker
Director of Production: Phillip Lee
Production Manager: Theresa L. Beste
Production Assistant: Faye Porter Bonner

Contributors:
Contributing Copy Editor and Technical Writer:
  Laura Morris Edwards
Contributing Photographer: Keith Harrelson
Contributing Photo Stylists: Connie Formby, Cathy Harris

Cover: *Old Timer,* page 8

Special thanks to the following who let us photograph quilts in their homes or businesses:
Ethan Allen Interiors, Vestavia, Alabama
Mr. and Mrs. Joe Harris, Birmingham, Alabama
Dr. and Mrs. Price Kloess, Mountain Brook, Alabama
Mr. and Mrs. Thomas L. Merrill, Sr., Mountain Brook, Alabama
Mr. and Mrs. John Simpson, Mountain Brook, Alabama
Mr. and Mrs. Tim Wamble, Homewood, Alabama

For more books to enrich your life, visit
oxmoorhouse.com

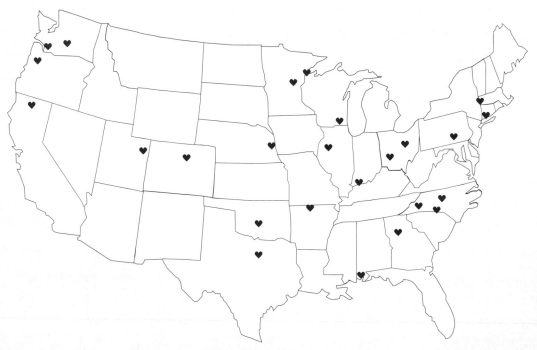

This year's edition of *Great American Quilts* features 25 quilters from 20 states, indicated in the map above.

From The Editor

Depression-era-style quilts continue to soar in popularity. Perhaps we are nostalgic for a time when people knew their neighbors and stretched a dime as far as it would go. Our own economic times require us to be more thrifty with our money than we were just a few years ago. Or perhaps we are drawn to the soft, pastel color palette and the whimsical conversational prints. Some quilters collect feedsacks from this period and make their quilts with fabrics authentic to the time, like Kathy Munkelwitz did with her quilt, *Nostalgia.* However, reproduction prints are plentiful. You can find the "Playtime" and "Home-Ec" lines from Michael Miller, the "Aunt Grace" fabrics by Judie Rothermel, the "30's Playtime" collection by Sharon Newman & Moda™, or the "Trip Around the World" prints by RJR Fabrics, shown on this page.

We celebrate this trend in our theme chapter, **Thrifty Thirties.** You'll find our cover quilt, *Old Timer,* along with a traditional favorite, *Rings of Hope. Sara's Garden* is a modern quilt with soft touches reminiscent of 1930s style, and *Grandmother's Flower Garden* is an actual antique from that era.

Quilts Across America features a sampling of quilts from coast to coast. *Hummingbird Heaven* and *Calico Rose* showcase fine appliqué and exquisite hand quilting. *Cherokee Heritage* celebrates Native American culture and design. If you're in the mood for a whimsical design, try *Pinwheels & Cherries* or *Target.*

Traditions in Quilting showcases traditional quilts with a modern twist. *Arachne* evolved from the classic Spider Web block, while *In My Garden: A Hummingbird Tale* consists of fine Feathered Stars. *Plaid Fantasy* combines the challenging Russian Sunflower and Tea Leaf blocks. *Spanish Tiles* features a scrappy collection of interlocking units, while *I'm in Love with Perry Winkle* has a monochromatic color scheme.

Bee Quilters features quilts made by quilting groups or duos. Some were made from block collections offered by friends, such as *Serendipity, Spring Has Sprung,* and *Beauty from Brokenness. Mediterranean Beauty* and *I Like Red* resulted from the collaborative efforts of a quiltmaker and a professional machine quilter.

Our **Designer Gallery** celebrates art quilts made by award-winning and nationally known quilt artists that have appeared in national shows. Although these one-of-a-kind quilts cannot be duplicated, let them inspire you to make your own masterpiece.

Rings of Hope, page 14

Target, page 50

Plaid Fantasy, page 92

Mediterranean Beauty, page 106

Bee Quilters

Designer Gallery

We Fix Broken Hearts, page 130

Thrifty Thirties

Doris R. Rogers
Mountain Home, Arkansas

Although there were no quilters in her family, Doris Rogers always knew that one day she would become a quilter. It finally happened in 1995. "My husband and I had recently retired and moved to Arkansas when he asked me to make something out of his ties," Doris recalls. "Some of his ties were from his college days. I used them to make a king-size Dresden Plate quilt that I finished in 1996. Then my dad gave me his ties, which dated back to the 1930s. I incorporated my dad's ties into a memory quilt for my parents. Making quilts for my family is very rewarding. Needless to say, I've been quilting ever since!"

Shortly after Doris moved to Arkansas, she joined the Hill 'n Hollow Quilters Guild. "I have been an active member since joining, and the friendships I have made are too numerous to count," says Doris.

"Making quilts is a way of expressing my love and preserving memories."

"A group of us called the Sew Whats meet regularly in each other's homes to exchange ideas and work on our current 'masterpiece.' We also go on quilt shop excursions and travel to quilt shows."

Doris is also a member of the American Quilter's Society. In 2002, she was honored by having *Old Timer* juried into the 18th annual quilt show and contest, where it won 2nd place in Mixed Techniques.

"I have found that my love of quilting is exciting and challenging, and an expression of my patience and attention to detail," says Doris. "Making quilts has strengthened my confidence and has enabled me to explore and develop new techniques. Also, making quilts is a way of expressing my love and preserving memories."

Old Timer
2001

Doris' love of old, traditional quilt patterns and her fabric collection inspired her to make *Old Timer*. "I was especially drawn to the Jack's Chain blocks because of the motion reflected in it," she says.

Doris used both hand- and machine-piecing in the quilt, but opted to hand-quilt the entire piece, which took about 15 months. "In order to finish the quilt for the guild's quilt show in October 2001, I hand-quilted eight to ten hours a day for the last four months!" she recalls. Luckily, Doris loves hand quilting and finds it relaxing.

All her hard work paid off. The quilt won ribbons for Best Application of Technical Skills and Viewers' Choice at the 2001 Hill 'n Hollow Show. It later appeared in The Great Arkansas Quilt Show in Little Rock, Arkansas, and was juried into the American Quilter's Society Show in 2002. There, it won a 2nd Place ribbon in Mixed Techniques, Amateur.

Old Timer

Finished Size
Quilt: 83½" x 91"

Materials
10–12 (⅜-yard) cuts assorted
    1930s prints (use more for
    greater variety)
10–15 fat eighths (9" x 22")
    assorted coordinating solids
7 yards white
3½ yards pale pink for borders
1 yard solid green for vine and
    leaves
1 yard total assorted green prints
    for leaves
1 fat eighth (9" x 22") mottled
    brown for vases
7½ yards fabric for backing
Queen-size batting

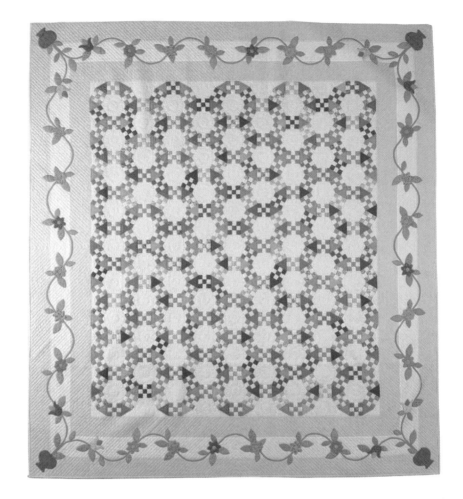

Cutting
Instructions are for rotary cutting and quick piecing. Cut
pieces in order listed to make
best use of yardage. Patterns are
on pages 12–13.

From assorted 1930s prints, cut:
- 10 assorted sets of 5 (1⅜"-
    wide) strips for Nine-Patch
    blocks.
- 4 yellow tulips E.
- 4 peach tulips E.
- 4 blue flowers F.
- 4 purple flowers F.
- 4 pink flowers F.
- 4 blue flowers G.
- 4 purple flowers G.
- 4 pink flowers G.

From assorted coordinating solids,
cut:
- 4 blue tulip centers D.
- 4 gold tulip centers D.
- 24 gold centers H.
- 190 assorted Bs.

From white, cut:
- 40 (1⅜"-wide) strips for Nine-
    Patch blocks.
- 85 As.
- 2⅝ yards. From yardage, cut
    4 (4½"-wide) lengthwise strips
    for borders.
- From remainder, cut 8 Cs, 8 Cs
    reversed, 16 side triangles (M),
    and 4 corner pieces (L).

From pale pink, cut:
- 10 (2¼"-wide) strips for binding.
- 2⅝ yards. From yardage, cut
    8 (4½"-wide) lengthwise strips
    for borders.

From solid green, cut:
- 4 (¾"-wide) bias strips, each
    102" long. Fold in thirds and
    press to make 4 (¼" x 102")
    bias strips for border vines.
- 16 large leaves J.
- 36 small leaves I.

From assorted green prints, cut:
- 45 large leaves J.
- 39 small leaves I.

From mottled brown, cut:
- 4 vases K.

Block Assembly
1. To make Nine-Patch units,
choose 4 white strips and 1 set of
5 print strips. Referring to *Strip
Set 1 Diagram*, join 2 print strips
to each side of 1 white strip to
make 1 Strip Set #1. Make 2 Strip
Sets #1. Cut Strip Sets #1 into 56
(1⅜"-wide) #1 segments.

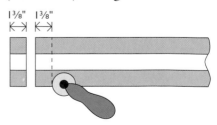

Strip Set 1 Diagram

2. Referring to *Strip Set 2 Diagram,* join 2 white strips to each long side of 1 print strip to make 1 Strip Set #2. Cut Strip Set #2 into 28 (1⅜"-wide) #2 segments.

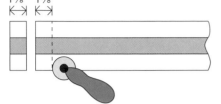

1⅜" 1⅜"

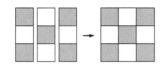

Strip Set 2 Diagram

3. Referring to *Nine-Patch Assembly Diagram,* lay out 2 #1 segments and 1 #2 segment as shown. Join to make 1 Nine-Patch unit. Make 28 Nine-Patch units.

Nine-Patch Assembly Diagram

4. Repeat Steps 1–3 to make 266 Nine-Patch units total.

5. Lay out 1 A, 6 assorted Bs, and 6 assorted Nine-Patch units as shown in *Block Assembly Diagram.* Join to make 1 Jack's Chain block *(Block Diagram).* Make 25 Jack's Chain blocks.

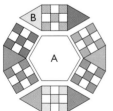

Block Assembly Diagram   *Block Diagram*

6. Lay out 1 A, 2 assorted Bs, and 4 assorted Nine-Patch units as shown in *Connector Block Assembly Diagram.* Join to make 1 connector block *(Connector Block Diagram).* Make 20 connector blocks.

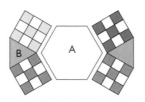

Connector Block Assembly Diagram

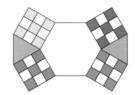

Connector Block Diagram

Quilt Assembly

1. Referring to *Quilt Top Assembly Diagram,* lay out 5 Jack's Chain blocks and 4 connector blocks as shown. Join to make 1 vertical block row. Make 5 vertical block rows.

2. Lay out 10 As and 9 Nine-Patch units. Join to make 1 vertical sashing row. Make 4 vertical sashing rows.

3. Alternate block rows and sashing rows. Join rows. Set in 4 Cs and 4 Cs reversed along top edge. Repeat for bottom edge. Set in 8 side triangles (M) on each side. Set in 4 corner pieces (L). Trim top and bottom As even with Cs.

4. Join 1 pink, 1 white, and 1 pink 4½"-wide strips to make 1 border strip. Make 4 border strips.

5. Center 1 border strip on each side of quilt and join. Miter corners.

6. Each side border has 1 vine, 1 peach tulip with gold center, 6 alternating G and F flowers in purple, pink and blue, all with gold centers, 1 yellow tulip with blue center, and leaves. See photo for placement of appliqués. Appliqué on border: 4 vines, 75 small leaves, 61 large leaves,

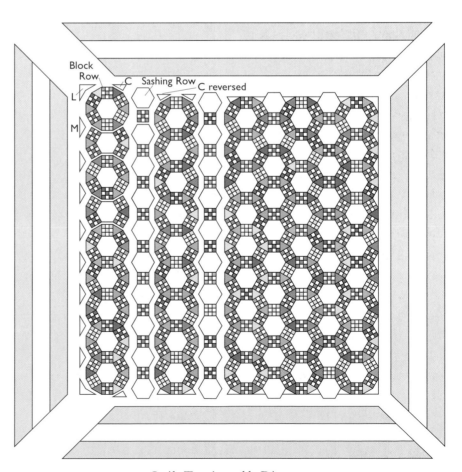

Quilt Top Assembly Diagram

4 blue tulip centers D, 4 yellow tulips E, 4 blue flowers F, 4 pink flowers G, 4 purple flowers F, 4 blue flowers G, 4 pink flowers F, 4 purple flowers G, 4 gold tulip centers D, 4 peach tulips E, 24 gold centers H, and 4 vases in corners.

Quilting and Finishing

1. Divide backing fabric into 3 (2½-yard) lengths. Cut 1 piece in half lengthwise. Sew 1 narrow panel between wide panels. Press seam allowances toward narrow panels. Remaining panel is extra and may be used to make a hanging sleeve. Seams will run horizontally.

2. Layer backing, batting, and quilt top; baste. Quilt as desired. Quilt shown is quilted in-the-ditch in Nine-Patch units, and is quilted ¼" inside triangles in coordinating thread. Block centers (A) have a wreath pattern. Border appliqué is outline-quilted, with diagonal fill for remainder of border.

3. Join 2¼"-wide pink strips into 1 continuous piece for straight-grain French-fold binding. Add binding to quilt.

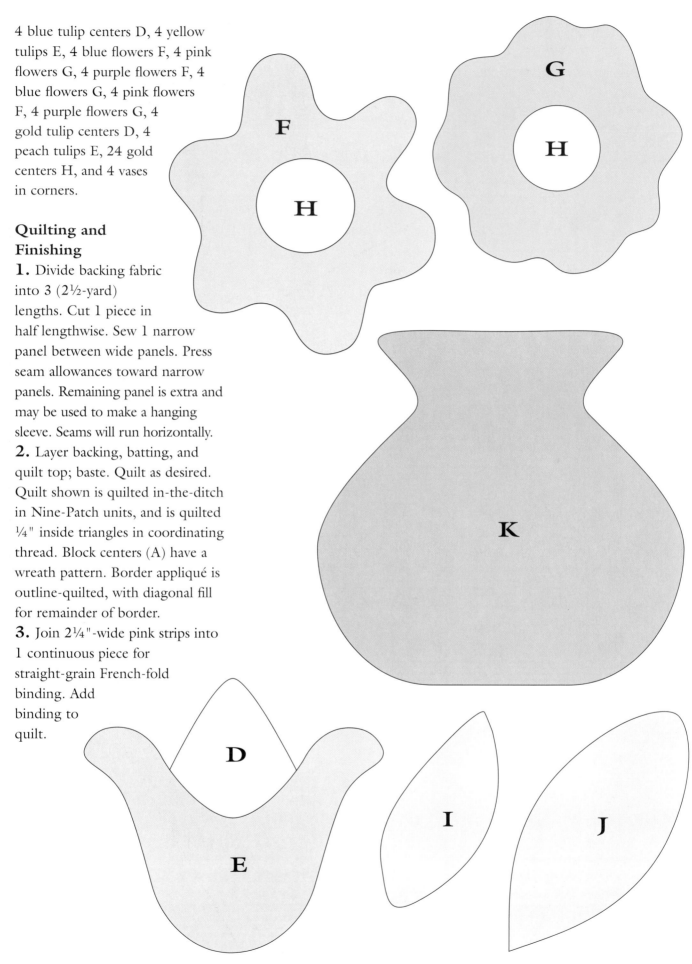

12

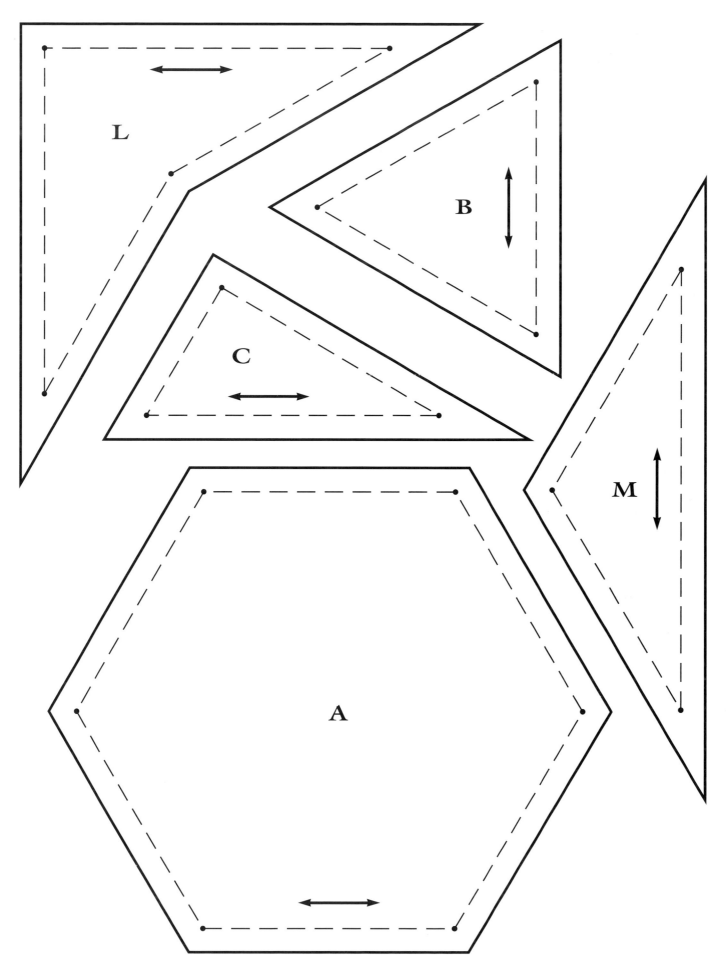

L

B

C

M

A

13

Linda Dyken
Mobile, Alabama

*L*inda Dyken has been quilting for more than 20 years. "I have always loved sewing garments, cross-stitch, rug hooking, embroidery, and crewel work, and I thought that quilting would be a combination of all the hobbies I enjoy," she says. "I started beginner classes in Augusta, Georgia. Then I moved to Mobile, Alabama, and joined the Azalea City Quilters Guild and signed up for every class that was offered. Pretty soon, I was addicted!"

Quilting plays a large role in Linda's life. "I usually quilt at least two hours a day," she says. "I find it gives me time to be contemplative and time to be expressive. Just to sit and think and stitch gives me joy and peace. I also find it very challenging, as each new project has problems to work out. It's really a constant learning and goal-reaching process."

"I find [that quilting] gives me time to be contemplative and time to be expressive. Just to sit and think and stitch gives me joy and peace."

Besides the relaxation and peace that quilting affords Linda, she also cherishes the friendships she has made through quilting. "I have made some wonderful friends who enjoy quilting as much as I do," she says.

Linda enjoys making quilts for her family. She strives to constantly improve her quilting stitches and to develop new quilting designs. "I like to quilt heavily by hand," she says.

Rings of Hope
2001

Linda Dyken became familiar with *Australian Patchwork & Quilting* magazine during her visit to Australia and New Zealand. A photo she saw in that magazine inspired her to start making a traditional Love Ring quilt.

"I started piecing the quilt by hand, and carried the pieces with me on many trips," Linda recalls. "I even pieced the rows together by hand."

Linda pieced the border first and then appliquéd it in place by hand. She used about 30 pieces from the Aunt Grace fabric line by Judie Rothermel, including yardage of one print for the backing. "I like the old-fashioned look," she says.

Since Linda finished the quilt two days after September 11, 2001, she named the quilt *Rings of Hope*. A few months later, it was juried into the 2002 American Quilter's Society Show in Paducah, Kentucky.

Rings of Hope

Finished Size

Quilt: 87" x 91"

Blocks: 338 (4") Drunkard's Path Blocks

Materials

5 yards assorted thirties prints

9 yards muslin

7⅞ yards fabric for backing

Queen-size batting

Cutting

From assorted thirties prints, cut:

• 490 As.

From muslin, cut:

• 2⅝ yards. From yardage, cut 4 (8"-wide) lengthwise strips for borders.

• 338 Bs.

• 4 (4½") squares for center.

• 10 (2¼"-wide) strips for binding.

Block Assembly

1. Referring to *Block Assembly Diagram*, join 1 print A and 1 muslin B to make 1 block.

2. Make 338 blocks.

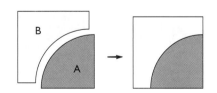

Block Assembly Diagram

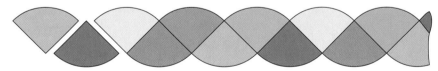

Border Assembly Diagram

Quilt Assembly

1. Lay out blocks and center squares in 19 rows of 18 blocks each as shown in *Quilt Top Assembly Diagram*. Join into rows; join rows to complete quilt center.

2. Center 1 border strip on each side of quilt and join. Miter corners.

3. Referring to *Border Assembly Diagram*, join 39 As to make 1 side appliqué border strip. Repeat. Join 37 As to make top appliqué border strip. Repeat for bottom border. Adjust seams as needed and appliqué to center of borders.

Quilting and Finishing

1. Divide backing fabric into 3 (2⅝-yard) lengths. Cut 1 piece in half lengthwise. Sew 1 narrow panel between wide panels. Press seam allowances toward narrow panel. Remaining panel is extra and may be used to make a hanging sleeve. Seams will run horizontally.

2. Layer backing, batting, and quilt top; baste. Quilt as desired. Quilt shown is grid-quilted in block background, with parallel curves through A pieces and border appliqué. Border background is filled with echo quilting.

3. Join 2¼"-wide muslin strips into 1 continuous piece for straight-grain French-fold binding. Add binding to quilt.

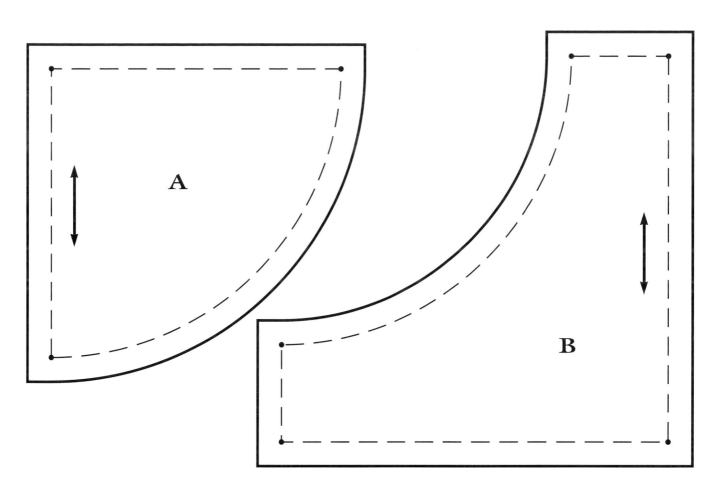

Quilt Top Assembly Diagram

Carol Matthews
Marietta, Georgia

Carol Matthews has had a love affair with fabric for as long as she can remember. As a young adult, she sewed for herself and for her home and dabbled in a variety of crafts. It wasn't until 1983, however, that her interests turned to quilting. "A neighbor of mine invited me to a meeting of quilters," Carol recalls. "This little group of quilters grew into the East Cobb Quilters Guild, which now boasts more than 250 members—and I am still one of them!" Carol is also a member of the Common Threads quilting bee.

Quilting became an important part of Carol's life shortly after her first quilt meeting. "My husband traveled a lot before he retired, and our boys were in school or involved with their own interests," Carol says. "I already had a sewing machine and a stash of fabric, so quilting just seemed a natural course to follow."

"I already had a sewing machine and a fabric stash, so quilting just seemed a natural course to follow."

Carol has made several quilts for the Ronald McDonald House and has sold several quilted items at a gift shop near her home. She also enjoys gardening and has recently tried her hand at ceramic mosaics. But her love of quilting will always come first.

Sara's Garden
2001

Carol Matthews had been working with dark fabrics for a good while when she came across the pink floral fabric she used in *Sara's Garden*. "I knew then that it was time to make a pastel quilt," Carol says.

However, a year passed before Carol found the floral companion prints to match the border fabric. Once she had her fabrics in hand, she got started.

"I love the old, traditional quilt blocks, and Churn Dash was one I had not used," Carol says. She decided to combine the blocks with several other techniques to give the quilt more visual appeal.

"I enjoy mixing appliqué and piecing," she says. "Since my color scheme was so spring-like, I just had to include some flowers in the design."

Sara's Garden was juried into the 2001 East Cobb Quilt Show in Atlanta, Georgia.

Sara's Garden

Finished Size
Quilt: 79" x 79"
Blocks: 12 (10") Churn Dash
Blocks

Materials
2 yards total assorted prints in
   4 color groups of green,
   purple, pink, and yellow for
   blocks and appliqué
4 yards white for blocks and border
2¾ yards pink print #1 for blocks
   and border
1½ yards pink print #2 for blocks
   and binding
1¾ yards purple stripe for inner
   border
1 yard green print #1 for wide vine
1 yard green print #2 for narrow
   vine
¼ yard light green print for leaves
4½ yards fabric for backing
Full-size batting
Embroidery floss in brown, green,
   and blue
Trapunto yarn or extra batting for
   stuffwork

Cutting
Instructions are for rotary cutting
and quick piecing. Cut pieces in
order listed to make best use of
yardage. Patterns are on pages
22–25.

From each of 4 color groups, cut:
- 6 (4⅞") squares. Cut squares in
  half diagonally to make 12 half-
  square triangles.
- 12–15 (2½") squares, depend-
  ing on whether you prefer white
  or print for center block
  squares.

From color group prints, cut:
- 4 A corner flower bases—2
  purple, 1 yellow, 1 pink
- 4 B corner flowers—2 purple,
  1 yellow, 1 pink.
- 4 C flower centers—solid yellow
- 3 butterflies—1 each pink,
  purple, and yellow. For each,
  cut 1 D wing, 1 D wing
  reversed, 1 lower wing E, and 1
  lower wing E reversed.
- 8 morning glories—3 purple,
  3 yellow, and 2 pink. Cut 6"
  circles and fold to center to
  make 2¼" wide hexagons. Tack
  center to hold.
- 8 yo-yos—3 yellow, 3 pink, and
  2 purple. Cut 3" circles. Fold in
  ¼" around edge and running
  stitch in place. Pull threads to
  gather yo-yo; arrange and press
  to make 1 yo-yo, 1¼" across.
  Appliqué in center of morning
  glory. Make 8 folded morning
  glories.
- F berries—10 pink, 6 yellow,
  and 9 purple.

From white, cut:
- 2¼ yards. From yardage, cut
  4 (10"-wide) lengthwise border
  strips.
- 3 (4⅞"-wide) strips. Cut strips
  into 24 (4⅞") squares. Cut
  squares in half diagonally to
  make 48 triangles for blocks.
- 4 (2½"-wide) strips. Cut strips
  into 48–60 (2½") squares for
  blocks and centers. Number
  depends on whether you choose
  to use white or print centers for
  blocks.
- 2 (10⅞"-wide) strips. Cut strips
  into 4 (10⅞") squares. Cut
  squares in half diagonally to
  make 8 triangles for half-
  triangle blocks.

- 1 (11¼"-wide) strip. Cut strip
  into 3 (11¼") squares. Cut
  squares in quarters diagonally to
  make 12 triangles for quarter
  triangle blocks. You will have
  2 extra.

From pink print #1, cut:
- 2¼ yards. From yardage, cut
  4 (10"-wide) lengthwise border
  strips.
- 2 (10⅞") squares. Cut squares
  in half diagonally to make 4
  triangles for corner half-triangle
  blocks.

From pink print #2, cut:
- 2 (10⅞") squares. Cut squares
  in half diagonally to make 4
  triangles for center half-triangle
  blocks.
- 3 (11¼") squares. Cut squares
  in quarters diagonally to make
  12 triangles for quarter-triangle
  blocks. You will have 2 extra.
- 9 (2¼"-wide) strips for binding.

From purple stripe, cut:
- 4 (2½"-wide) lengthwise strips
  for inner border.

From green print #1, cut:
- 325" of 1½"-wide bias strip.
  Fold and press to make 325"
  of ½"-wide bias for wide vine.
  Cut 4 (4½"-long) sections for
  corner stems.
- 36 large leaves G.

From green print #2, cut:
- 300" of ¾"-wide bias strip.
  Fold and press to make 300" of
  ¼"-wide bias for narrow vine.
- 11 small leaves I.
- 8 leaves J.
- 4 leaves J reversed.

From light green print, cut:
- 16 large leaves G.
- 8 small leaves H.

Block Assembly

1. Choose 1 color group of 4 triangles and 4 squares. Referring to *Corner Unit Assembly Diagram*, join 1 white and 1 print triangle to make 1 cor-

Corner Unit Assembly Diagram

ner unit. Make 4 corner units. Referring to *Side Unit Assembly Diagram*, join 1 white and 1 print squares to make 1 side unit. Make 4 side units.

Side Unit Assembly Diagram

2. Referring to *Block Assembly Diagram*, lay out corner units and side units with 1 center square. Join into rows; join rows to complete 1 Churn Dash block (*Block Diagram*).

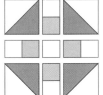
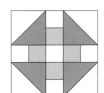

Block Assembly Diagram   *Block Diagram*

3. Make 12 Churn Dash blocks, 3 in each color group. Center squares may be white or print as you choose.

4. Join 2 pink print #2 and 2 white triangles as shown in *Quarter-Block Assembly Diagram* to make 1 quarter-triangle block. Make 5 quarter-triangle blocks.

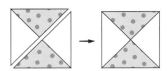

Quarter-Block Assembly Diagram

5. Join 1 pink print #2 and 1 white triangles as shown in

Half-Block Assembly Diagram to make 1 half-block. Make 4 half-triangle blocks with pink print #2 for center and 4 half-triangle blocks with pink print #1 for corners.

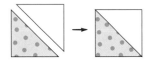

Half-Block Assembly Diagram

Quilt Assembly

1. Lay out blocks as shown in *Quilt Top Assembly Diagram*. Join into rows; join rows to complete quilt center.

2. Center 1 purple inner border on each side of quilt and join. Miter corners.

3. Baste 1 pink print border to 1 white border strip, overlapping by 5" to make 1 (13"-wide) border. Make 4 borders. Using curve

pattern on page 25, mark scallops evenly on pink border and appliqué to white border (*Border Assembly Diagram*). Trim white from behind appliqué. Center border strips and join to quilt, matching appliqué and mitering corners.

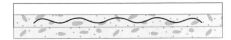

Border Assembly Diagram

4. Using patterns on pages 22–25 and referring to *Appliqué Assembly Diagram* on page 25, position wide green vines, narrow green vines, and corner stems on border. When satisfied with placement, appliqué. Add leaves and corner flower units. Add butterflies and berries. Embroider details and stuff berries if desired. Add folded morning glories.

Quilt Top Assembly Diagram

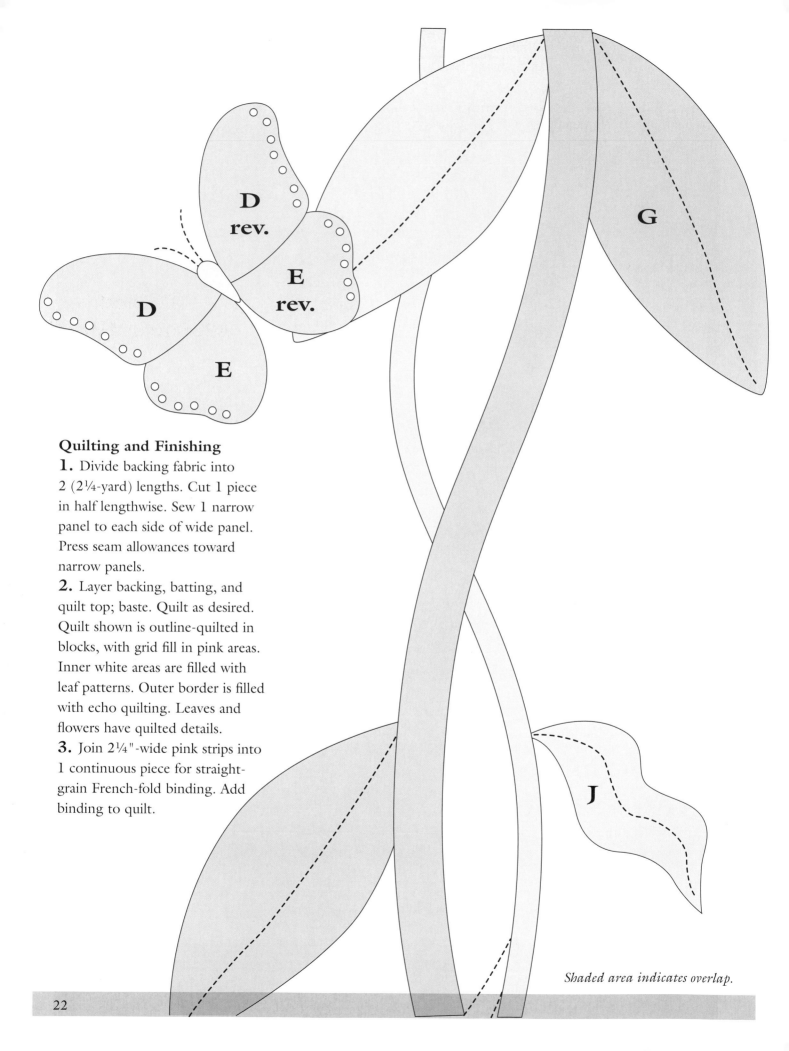

Quilting and Finishing

1. Divide backing fabric into 2 (2¼-yard) lengths. Cut 1 piece in half lengthwise. Sew 1 narrow panel to each side of wide panel. Press seam allowances toward narrow panels.

2. Layer backing, batting, and quilt top; baste. Quilt as desired. Quilt shown is outline-quilted in blocks, with grid fill in pink areas. Inner white areas are filled with leaf patterns. Outer border is filled with echo quilting. Leaves and flowers have quilted details.

3. Join 2¼"-wide pink strips into 1 continuous piece for straight-grain French-fold binding. Add binding to quilt.

D rev.

E rev.

D

E

G

J

Shaded area indicates overlap.

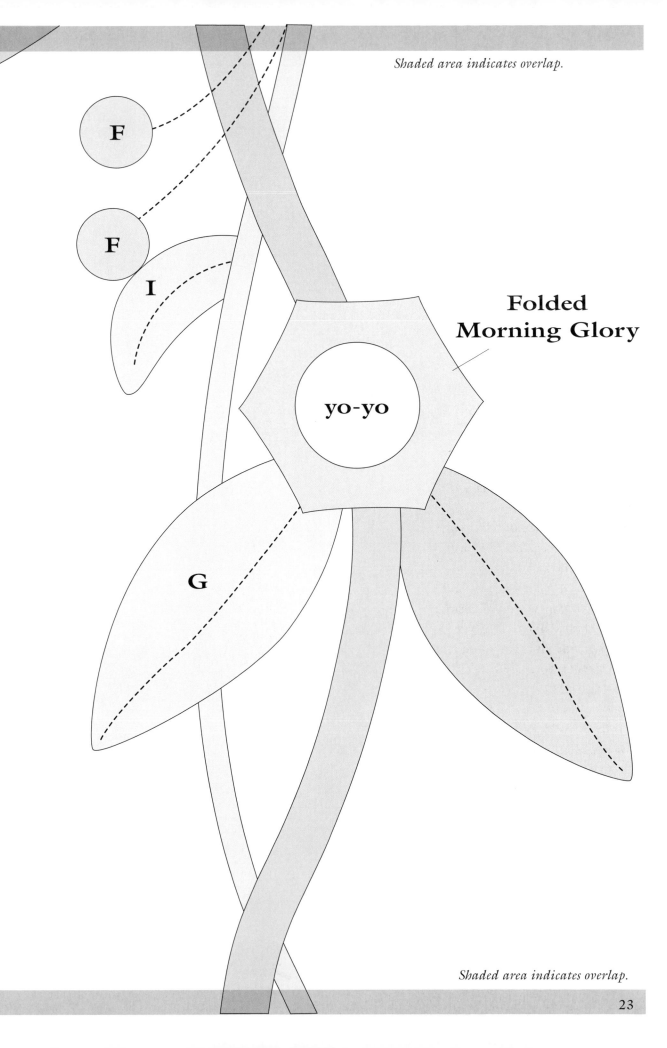

F

F

I

yo-yo

G

**Folded
Morning Glory**

Shaded area indicates overlap.

Shaded area indicates overlap.

G

H

A

B

C

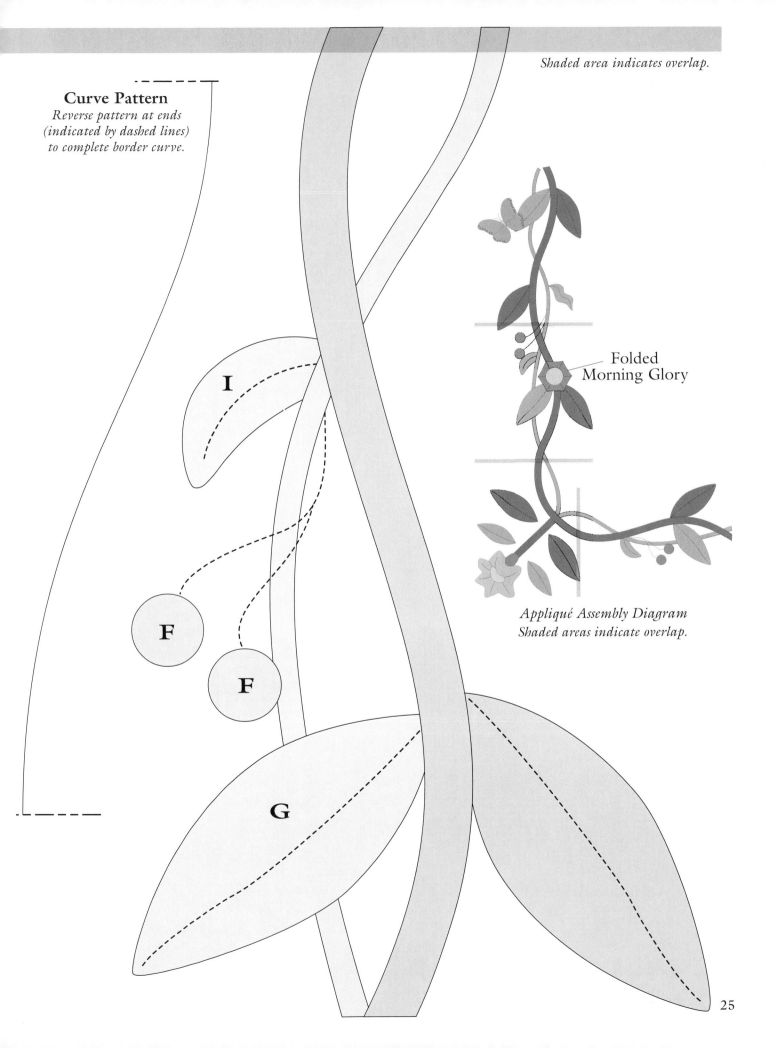

Shaded area indicates overlap.

Curve Pattern
*Reverse pattern at ends
(indicated by dashed lines)
to complete border curve.*

I

Folded
Morning Glory

*Appliqué Assembly Diagram
Shaded areas indicate overlap.*

F

F

G

25

Judy Howard
Oklahoma City, Oklahoma

*J*udy Howard has owned and operated Buckboard Antiques and Quilts for more than 28 years. She started her antique business in a small 1920s cottage just north of the Oklahoma State Fairgrounds.

Judy's love of quilts developed while taking a class from renowned fiber artist Terrie Mangat. A charter member of the Oklahoma Quilt Guild, Judy's quilting friends and faithful clients quickly multiplied. Judy began offering quilt classes, and antique quilts became her specialty as her shop expanded to 10 rooms.

"Working and living with these art forms is so stimulating," says Judy, who is also surrounded at home with her own personal collection of quilts. "And I have such fun assisting others in the selection of a perfect handmade quilt for a wedding, anniversary, or birthday gift. Coordinating a legacy heirloom with someone's personal decorating taste is a joy."

"Coordinating a legacy heirloom with someone's personal decorating taste is a joy."

Julia Roberts, star of *America's Sweethearts,* likes to give Wedding Ring quilts for wedding gifts. Judy's other celebrity clients include Jessica Lange and Dustin Hoffman, who purchased 17 quilts while in town to film *Rainman.*

Judy's mail order business offers photos of 250 antique quilts, quilt tops, and quilt blocks, as well as hand-hooked rugs, crocheted bedspreads, and Pendleton blankets. You can visit her Web site at www.buckboardquilts.com.

Grandmother's Flower Garden
circa 1930

The small pieces of this authentic 1930s quilt made it an ideal choice for frugal quilters working with scraps. "This *Grandmother's Flower Garden* is superb in its artistic appeal because of its bright colors, dynamic design, and expert workmanship," says Judy. "Gardens were the focal point of color on every homestead. No wonder this design is so popular and meaningful today as Americans are returning to home comfort and their own backyard gardens for beauty."

Quilter Belle Wilson, who lived from 1860 to 1943, made this quilt. She arrived in Hunter, Oklahoma in a covered wagon.

"Belle would have worked from dawn to dusk on the farm growing cotton to make her own batting," says Judy. "She no doubt pieced it while rocking on the hot porch during the summer sunsets and hand-quilted it snuggled by the fireside with a kerosene lamp during bitter prairie winters."

Grandmother's Flower Garden

Finished Size

Quilt: 73" x 99½"
Blocks: 60 (9⅝" x 10⅝")
Grandmother's Flower Garden
Blocks

Materials

¾ yard solid yellow for block centers
7½ yards white for path and borders
1½ yards assorted solids in pinks
    and reds for blocks
¾ yard green print for blocks
2½ yards total assorted prints for
    blocks
¾ yard solid pink for border
1 yard solid pink for binding
5¾ yards fabric for backing
Queen-size batting
Freezer paper for templates

Cutting

Cut pieces in order listed to
make best use of yardage.
Pattern is on page 30.
From yellow, cut:
• 178 As.
From white, cut:
• 2⅝ yards. Cut yardage into
    4 (5½"-wide) lengthwise strips.
    Trim strips to make 2 (5½" x
    90") outer side borders and
    2 (5½" x 73½") outer top and
    bottom borders. Cut yardage
    into 2 (6½"-wide) lengthwise
    strips. Trim to make 2 (6½" x
    75") inner side borders.
• 3 (6½"-wide) strips. Piece to
    make 2 (6½" x 60½") top and
    bottom inner borders.
• 1144 As.
From assorted solids, cut:
• 60 sets of 6 As.

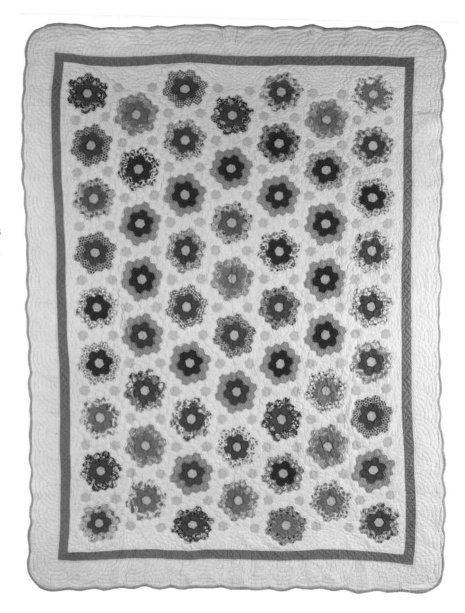

From green print, cut:
• 12 sets of 12 As.
From assorted prints, cut:
• 48 sets of 12 As.
From pink, cut:
• 8 (2"-wide) strips for border.
    Piece to make 2 (2" x 60½")
    top and bottom borders and
    2 (2" x 90") side borders.

Block Assembly

See page 31 for English paper-
piecing instructions.
1. Referring to *Assorted Print
Block Diagram*, join 6 pink or red
solid As to 1 yellow A as shown to

form small flower. Add 12 print As
to make a larger flower. Surround
flower with 18 white As to complete block. Make 48 assorted
print blocks.

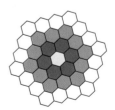

*Assorted Print
Block Assembly Diagram*

2. Referring to *Green Block
Diagram*, join 6 pink or red solid
As to 1 yellow A as shown to form

small flower. Add 12 As in green print to make a larger flower. Surround flower with 18 white As to complete block. Make 12 green blocks.

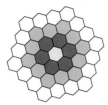

Green Block Assembly Diagram

Quilt Assembly

1. Referring carefully to *Row Assembly Diagram,* lay out assorted print blocks and green blocks as shown. (Note that green blocks form a subtle Flower Garden block design.) Fill in corners as shown with yellow As. (Note the odd angles; the setting will not work if you try to "straighten" the rows.) Join into rows; join rows.

2. Join top and bottom inner borders to inner side borders to make inner border frame for appliqué *(Frame Diagram).*

3. Add top and bottom pink borders. Add side pink borders.

4. Add white side outer borders. Add white top and bottom outer borders.

5. Center flower section on inner border frame as shown in *Quilt Top Assembly Diagram,* and appliqué in place. Remove paper to complete quilt. Trim inner border behind appliqué if desired.

Quilting and Finishing

1. Divide backing fabric into 2 (2⅞-yard) lengths. Cut 1 piece in half lengthwise. Sew 1 narrow panel to each side of wide panel. Press seam allowances toward narrow panels.

Row Assembly Diagram

Frame Diagram

2. Layer backing, batting, and quilt top; baste. Quilt as desired. Quilt shown is quilted in concentric circles by the piece in each flower. Pink border has a braid pattern, and outer border is quilted in Baptist fans.

3. Make 10 yards of 2¼"-wide bias strip from pink binding fabric. Fold and press to make bias French-fold binding. Add binding to quilt following fan pattern to form scallops. Trim scallops and turn binding to back to complete.

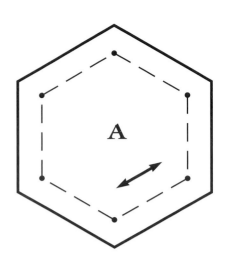

Quilt Top Assembly Diagram

English Paper Piecing

1. Using template on page 30, trace and cut paper templates without seam allowances from freezer paper. You will need 2,402 hexagons for quilt shown.

2. To cut several shapes quickly, fan-fold the freezer paper to create several layers. Trace template on top layer only. Pin or staple all layers together to keep them from shifting. Cut out templates through all layers *(Photo A)*.

3. With shiny side of freezer paper against wrong side of fabric, press paper templates to fabrics, using dry iron and wool setting. Make sure fabric pieces are at least ¼" larger than templates. Use rotary cutter and ruler to cut out hexagons ¼" from paper edge *(Photo B)*.

4. With paper side up, fold seam allowance over paper edge. Baste seam allowance to wrong side, stitching through paper *(Photo C)*. *Note: We used contrasting thread for clarity in photos, but you will want to use matching thread.*

5. With right sides facing and folded edges aligned, whipstitch pieces together. Pull thread through and reinsert needle in fold next to previous stitch, looping thread over folded edges *(Photo D)*. Make tiny stitches, ¹⁄₁₆" to ⅛" apart, and sew from corner to corner. Knot thread or backstitch to secure ends.

6. Remove basting stitches and freezer paper when all edges are stitched. Leave paper in edge pieces until appliquéd to inner borders.

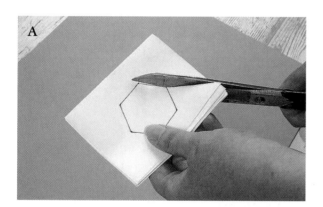

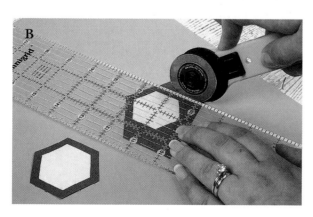

Kathy Munkelwitz
Isle, Minnesota

Kathy Munkelwitz began quilting in 1976. Her mother-in-law had been making a quilt for one of Kathy's daughters, but she passed away before the quilt was finished. Kathy wanted to finish the quilt, so her own mother showed her how. That was the beginning of what was to become a great passion for Kathy.

"It snowballed from there," Kathy recalls. "I think whenever you go into something because of a love for it, it's because everything about it grabs you and pulls you in. The feel of the fabric, the patterns on them, the spools of colored thread, the steady purr of the sewing machine—it's comforting and soothing. You know you're hooked when you see a piece of fabric and you think, 'I can't live without that piece!'"

Kathy and her husband Alton have a farm near Isle, Minnesota. For two months each spring, they devote their time to the sheep, for that's when they lamb each year. And when a mare is foaling, Kathy stops what she's doing to attend to the mother and the new foal. The rest of the time, you can usually find Kathy quilting.

"I still like my quilts to be functional, washable—something you want to wrap around yourself."

Kathy's best-known work stems from her quilts made from authentic feed-sacks. "I'm really drawn to them," she confesses. "They are sometimes stained, are different textures and weights—and therefore hard to handle—but I just love them. Maybe it's the oldness of it, the bygone days aspect. Or maybe it's because you're stuck with what you have—you can't go out and buy more."

Nostalgia
2002

Kathy Munkelwitz designed this quilt based on the traditional Economy block. "It's an interesting block that could be used several ways," says Kathy. "I just used what I had." Her make-do spirit echoes that of thrifty quilters from the 1930s.

To add to the quilt's antique look, Kathy used a cotton batt and added some extra padding under some of the quilting designs (also known as trapunto). Once completed, she washed the quilt to give it a well-loved look.

Kathy's work has been published in numerous books and magazines, and she has won many national quilting awards.

She finished *Nostalgia* just in time to appear in *Great American Quilts 2004*.

"I'm really a traditional quilter," Kathy says. "At shows, a lot of new, contemporary styles are popular. But I still like my quilts to be functional, washable—something you want to wrap around yourself."

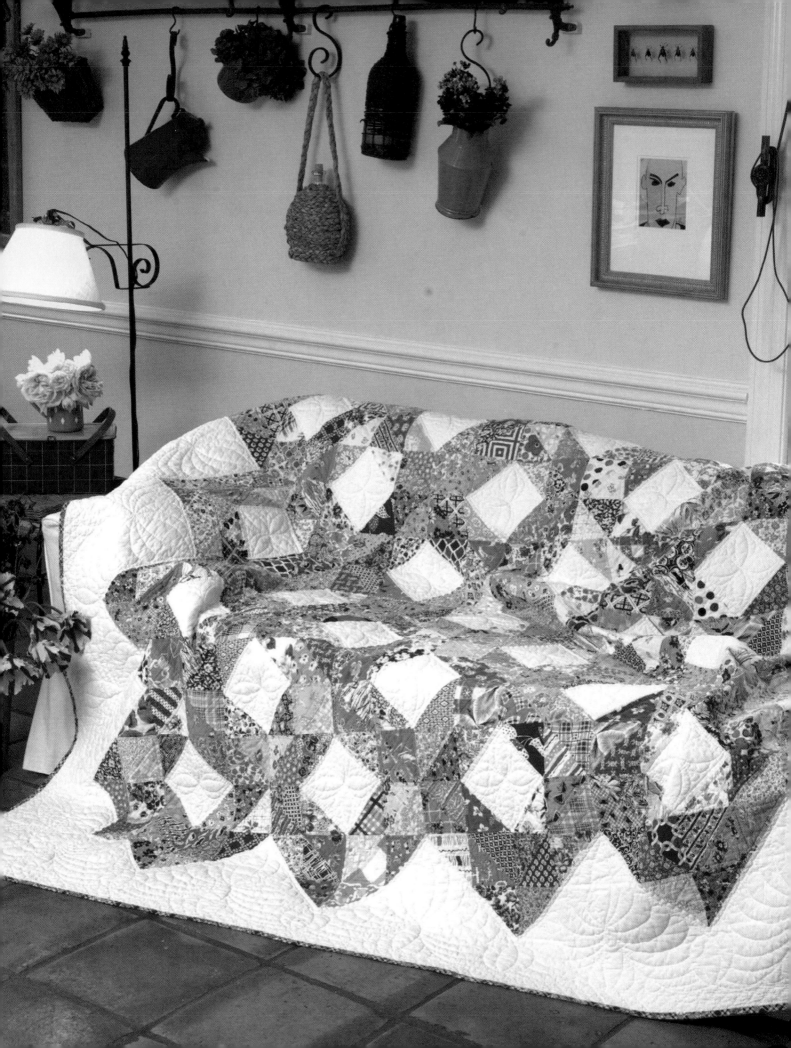

Nostalgia

Finished Size

Quilt: 87½" x 104½"
Blocks: 32 (11½") Economy
Blocks

Materials

5½ yards white fabric
6 yards total assorted feedsack prints
¾ yard fabric for binding
7⅞ yards fabric for backing
Queen-size batting

Cutting

Instructions are for rotary cutting and quick piecing. Cut pieces in order listed to make best use of yardage.

From white fabric, cut:

- 3 yards. Cut yardage into 4 (6"-wide) lengthwise strips for borders.
- From lengthwise remainder, cut 32 (6½") squares for block centers.
- 11 (4¾"-wide) strips. Cut strips into 22 (4¾" x 17½") rectangles for border pieces.
- 1 (9¾"-wide) strip. Cut strip into 4 (9¾") squares. Cut squares in quarters diagonally to make 16 side unit triangles. You will have 2 extra.

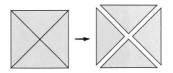

Quarter-Square Cutting Diagram

From assorted feedsack prints, cut:

- 121 (7¼") squares. Cut squares in quarters diagonally to make 484 quarter-square triangles for blocks.
- 36 (4¾") squares for border.

From binding fabric, cut:

- 11 (2¼"-wide) strips for binding.

Block Assembly

1. Join 1 triangle to each side of 1 block center as shown in *Block Assembly Diagram*. Join 2 triangles to make 1 block corner. Make 4 block corners. Add block corners to complete 1 block.

2. Make 32 blocks.

3. Referring to *Side Unit Assembly Diagram*, join 1 triangle to each short side of 1 side unit triangle. Add 1 triangle to each previous triangle as shown. Join 2 triangles to make 1 corner. Add corner to complete 1 side unit. Make 14 side units.

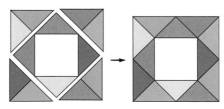

Block Assembly Diagram

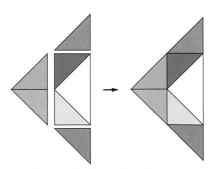

Side Unit Assembly Diagram

4. Referring to *Corner Unit Assembly Diagram*, join 4 triangles as shown to make 1 corner unit. Make 4 corner units.

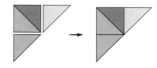

Corner Unit Assembly Diagram

5. Referring to *Border Unit Assembly Diagram*, place 1 print square atop 1 rectangular border strip, right sides facing. Stitch diagonally from corner to corner. Trim excess fabric ¼" from stitch-

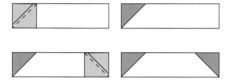

Border Unit Assembly Diagram

ing. Press open to reveal triangle. Repeat on opposite end to make 1 border unit, orienting triangles as shown. Make 14 border units with triangles on both ends, 4 border units with 1 triangle on right end, and 4 border units with 1 triangle on left end.

Quilt Assembly

1. Lay out blocks and units as shown in *Quilt Top Assembly Diagram*. Join into diagonal rows; join rows to complete quilt center.
2. Join 3 border units plus 1 right and 1 left border unit as shown. Match seams of triangles to top of quilt and add. Repeat for bottom border.
3. Join 4 border units plus 1 right and 1 left border unit. Match

seams of triangles to sides of quilt and add. Repeat for opposite side. Miter corners.
4. Center 1 border strip on each side of quilt and add. Miter corners.

Quilting and Finishing

1. Divide backing fabric into 3 (2⅝-yard) lengths. Join along sides to make backing. Seams will run horizontally.
2. Layer backing, batting, and quilt top; baste. Quilt as desired. Quilt shown is outline-quilted in triangles, with an orange peel pattern in centers. Border is filled with feather plumes and diagonals.
3. Join 2¼"-wide binding strips into 1 continuous piece for straight-grain French-fold binding. Add binding to quilt.

Quilt Top Assembly Diagram

Quilts Across America

Kathryn Rouse
Racine, Wisconsin

When her best friend was having a baby in the early 1980s, Kathryn Rouse decided that a baby quilt would be the perfect gift. "Although I knew nothing about making quilts, I made a tied comforter using pastel ginghams in a Log Cabin design," Kathryn recalls. "It was far from perfect, but she was delighted, and her son loved it and used it for many years."

When Kathryn left her teaching career a year later, she took a sampler quilting class. She learned many new techniques and began making quilts from commercial patterns. "But after entering a quilt in the American Quilter's Society Show and having it rejected because someone else submitted an identical quilt, I decided it was time to design something original," she says. Since then, all of her quilts have been original designs. In 1994, she was the $10,000 Grand Prize winner of the Lands End/Good Housekeeping Great American Quilt Contest.

"Quilting has been a wonderful hobby and creative outlet for me," Kathryn says. "Unlike clothing, which no matter how beautifully made is eventually discarded, quilts last for generations. Although I love seeing wall quilts and smaller projects that many quilters make, I've chosen to limit myself to making bed-size quilts. Since I fit my quilting in between volunteer work, gardening, traveling, and family responsibilities, a quilt may take me three years to complete. It's a long time, but I have a strong sense of accomplishment at the end, and it's worth it to me."

> *"A quilt may take me three years to complete. It's a long time, but I have a strong sense of accomplishment...and it's worth it to me."*

Pinwheels and Cherries
2001

A renewed interest in four-block quilts led Kathryn Rouse to design *Pinwheels and Cherries*. "I enjoy patterns with movement, and the cherries make the pinwheels appear to swirl. Also, one of the pinwheels spins in the opposite direction."

Kathryn designed the border to complement the four blocks.

"The narrow dogtooth borders were fun to make. They add interest to the design and stabilize the edges."

Also noteworthy is Kathryn's exquisite hand quilting. "I love the simplicity of echo quilting, in that I don't have to mark the quilting design. But I drew in a few additional shapes for fun.

Hand-quilting the rows ¼" apart is *very* time consuming, but to me, it is one of the most important elements of a beautiful quilt."

Pinwheels and Cherries was juried into the 2002 American Quilter's Society Show in Paducah, Kentucky, and won the Viewer's Choice Award at the 2002 Wandering Foot Quilters Show.

Pinwheels and Cherries

Finished Size
Quilt: 84" x 84"
Blocks: 4 (30") Blocks

Materials
8¼ yards unbleached muslin
1½ yards blue print for triangles
    and binding
1 fat quarter blue print for blocks
1 yard total assorted red prints for
    blocks, cherries, and border
    flowers
1 yard total assorted yellow prints
    for blocks and border flowers
2 yards total assorted green prints
    for blocks, stems, and border
    leaves
1 yard brown print for vine
½ yard total assorted brown prints
    for blocks and flower bases
7½ yards fabric for backing
Queen-size batting

Cutting
Instructions are for rotary cutting and quick piecing. Cut pieces in order listed to make best use of yardage. Border strips are exact length needed. You may want to cut them longer to allow for piecing variations. Patterns are on pages 42–43.

From unbleached muslin, cut:
- 4 (30½"-wide) strips. Cut strips into 4 (30½") appliqué background squares.
- 1¾ yards. Cut yardage into 2 (12½"-wide) lengthwise strips. Cut strips into 2 (12½" x 60½") side borders.
- 2½ yards. Cut yardage into 2 (12½"-wide) lengthwise

strips. Cut strips into 2 (12½" x 84½") top and bottom borders.

From first blue print (1½ yards), cut:
- 6 (4¼"-wide) strips. Cut strips into 46 (4¼") squares. Cut squares in quarters diagonally to make 184 border triangles E.
- From remainder, cut 4 (2⅜") squares. Cut squares in half diagonally to make 8 corner triangles F.
- 9 (2¼"-wide) strips for binding.

From second blue print (fat quarter), cut:
- 2 As.
- 1 set of 12 C triangles.
- 2 Bs.

From assorted red prints, cut:
- 1 set of 12 C triangles.
- 48 D cherries for blocks.
- 12 large cherries for border.
- 10 border flowers.
- 10 Bs.

From assorted yellow prints, cut:
- 2 sets of 12 C triangles.
- 1 A.
- 9 Bs.
- 10 border flowers.

From assorted green prints, cut:
- 480" of 1⅛"-wide bias strips. Fold in thirds and press to make bias. Cut folded bias into 64 (⅜" x 5") short stems for blocks and border. Cut bias into 16 (⅜" x 9") long stems for blocks.
- 20 leaves.
- 16 leaves reversed.
- 8 Bs.

From one brown print, cut:
- 350" of 1½"-wide bias strip. Fold in thirds and press to make ½"-wide bias strip for border vine.

From assorted brown prints, cut:
- 1 A.
- 3 Bs.
- 20 flower bases.

Block Assembly

1. Because triangles will be appliquéd to 2 sides of each block at a later stage, the main appliqué motif has to be slightly off-center. To do this, fold background square in quarters to make placement creases (shown in dashed lines). Referring to *Appliqué Background Diagram*, use a pencil or water-soluble pen to draw a line ¾" to the right of the vertical line and ¾" below the horizontal line (shown in solid lines) for appliqué placement lines. Tie a pencil to a tack with a 7¾" string between the two (or use a compass), and draw a circle for appliqué placement lines. **Tip:** It might be helpful to mark which 2 sides will have triangles appliquéd later, so that you don't turn the blocks the wrong way later.

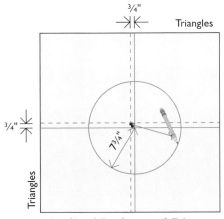

Appliqué Background Diagram

2. Center 1 A on background square. Appliqué in place. Position and appliqué 8 assorted Bs, referring to photo for colors and placement.

3. Position and baste 4 long and 8 short bias stems. Position and baste 12 C triangles. Appliqué stems and then triangles in place. Appliqué 12 D cherries to complete 1 Pinwheels and Cherries block.

4. Make 4 Pinwheels and Cherries blocks in color combinations shown. Note that in lower right block, the pinwheel spins in the opposite direction. You may replicate this look or have your pinwheels all spin in the same direction.

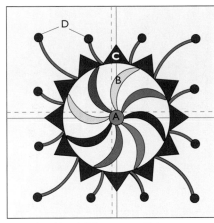

Appliqué Placement Diagram

Quilt Assembly

1. Lay out blocks as shown in *Quilt Top Assembly Diagram*, making sure "short" sides are in the center. Join into rows; join rows.

2. Appliqué 19 border triangles (E) on each side, centering on seam line. Raw edge may be basted in place. Appliqué 1 corner triangle (F) in each corner.

3. Add side borders to quilt. Add top and bottom borders. Raw edges of border triangles will be enclosed in the seams.

4. Referring to photo, appliqué 27 border triangles (E) to each side. Raw edge may be basted in place. Appliqué 1 corner triangle (F) in each corner.

5. Position brown vine as shown on border. Pin in place. Position green stems and leaves, slipping

Quilt Top Assembly Diagram

ends under vine. Appliqué. *Note:* Leaves are on outside of vine and reversed leaves are to inside of vine.

6. Appliqué 20 flowers, 20 flower bases, and 12 large cherries onto border as shown in photo.

Quilting and Finishing

1. Divide backing fabric into 3 (2½-yard) lengths. Cut 1 piece in half lengthwise. Sew 1 narrow panel between wide panels. Press seam allowances toward narrow panel. Remaining panel is extra and may be used to make a hanging sleeve. Seams will run horizontally.

2. Layer backing, batting, and quilt top; baste. Quilt as desired. Quilt shown is closely channel-quilted, with the addition of leaves and teardrops in borders and blocks.

3. Join 2¼"-wide blue print strips into 1 continuous piece for straight-grain French-fold binding. Add binding to quilt.

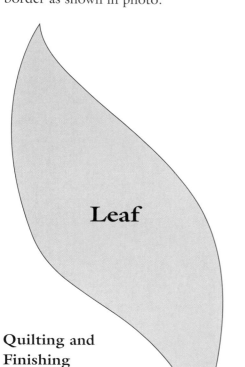

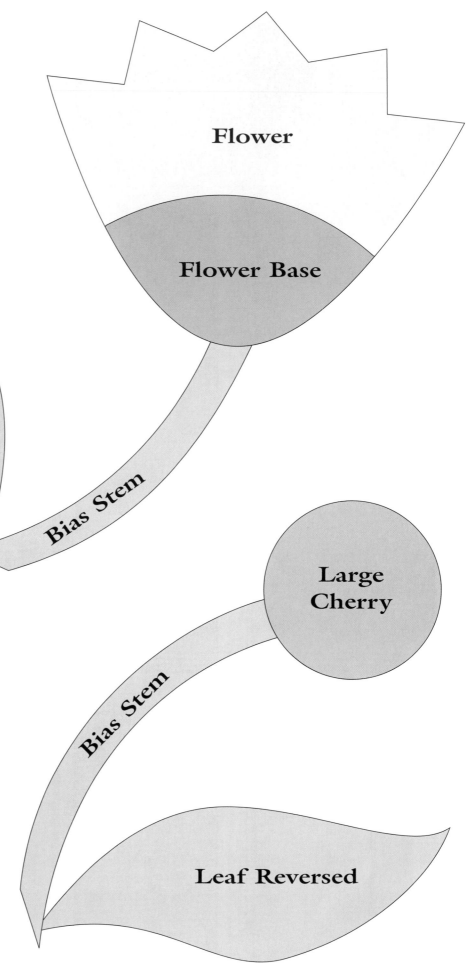

42

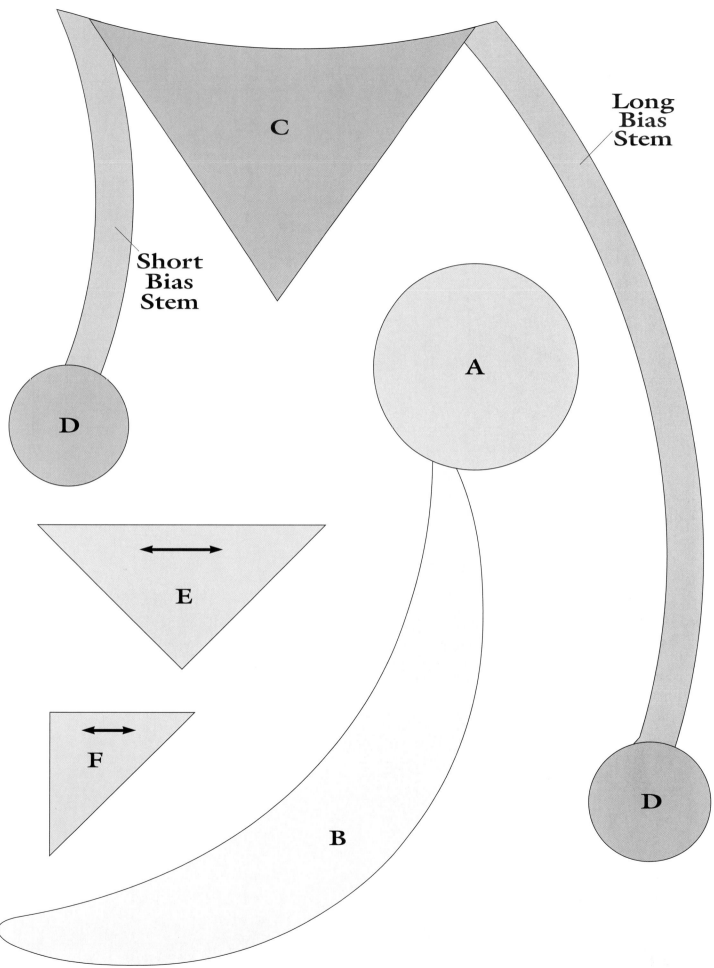

Long
Bias
Stem

Short
Bias
Stem

C

A

D

E

F

B

D

Jean Lohmar
Galesburg, Illinois

Jean Lohmar has always been fascinated by the sewing machine. "When my children were growing up, I made most of their clothing and mine," she recalls. "I worked for 20 years in a local shop, selling machines and teaching customers how to use them. I was a hand-quilter for most of 30 years, so it seemed natural to me to combine the two when I discovered Harriet Hargrave's machine quilting booklet."

Jean is a member of several quilt guilds and organizations, including the Piecemaker's Quilt Guild of Galesburg, Illinois; the Mississippi Valley Quilt Guild of Davenport, Iowa; the National Quilt Association; the American Quilter's Society; and the International Quilt Association.

Jean's exquisite machine quilting has been a source of enjoyment for her entire family. "All of our grandchildren have received specially-made quilts to take to college when they graduated high school," she says. "I just finished the fifth one for Ben, who was born on my birthday."

"I find [quilting] to be a source of inner peace and quiet time, and I am proud that I am leaving a legacy for my family."

Both Jean and her husband are retired and spend most of their time traveling to visit their 7 children and 13 grandchildren. "I always take some stage of quilting with me," Jean says. "I find it to be a source of inner peace and quiet time, and I am proud that I am leaving a legacy for my family."

Hummingbird Heaven
2001

Hummingbird Heaven is Jean Lohmar's adaptation of the traditional cockscomb pattern. "I like the visual impact of the reds and greens in those old 1800s quilts," says Jean. "When I found this combination of fabrics in batiks, I knew a new quilt was on the way."

Freezer-paper appliqué is Jean's preferred method of appliqué, because she can do all the preparation work of cutting and gluing while she travels. "From past experience, I know I never sleep on planes," says Jean. "So I cut and glued all of the pieces—including the 396 red berries—on our travels to and from Scandinavia."

Hummingbird Heaven is machine-constructed and machine-quilted, including the trapunto work. It was juried into the 2002 Heritage Quilt Show in Lancaster, Pennsylvania. It won Honorable Mention at the 2002 American Quilter's Society Show in Paducah, Kentucky. It took home 1st Place at Quilt America in Indianapolis, Indiana.

Hummingbird Heaven

Finished Size

Quilt: 89" x 89"
Blocks: 13 (16½") Blocks

Materials

8 yards light pink-and-green batik
    for background and border
2 yards bright print for leaves and
    piping
1 fat eighth (9" x 22") purple print
    for centers
2½ yards dark green print for
    flower bases, leaves, binding,
    and piping
1 yard red/orange print for flowers
¾ yard red print for berries
¾ yard green batik for stems
7⅞ yards fabric for backing
Queen-size batting
22 yards of 1/16"-diameter string for
    piping

Cutting

Instructions are for rotary cutting and quick piecing. Cut pieces in order listed to make best use of yardage. Patterns are on pages 48–49.

From light pink-and-green batik, cut:

• 2⅝ yards. Cut yardage into 4 (10"-wide) lengthwise strips for border strips.
• 7 (17"-wide) strips. Cut strips into 13 (17") squares for backgrounds.
• 2 (25"-wide) strips. Cut strips into 2 (25") squares. Cut squares in quarters diagonally to make 8 side setting triangles.
• From remainder, cut 2 (13") squares. Cut squares in half diagonally to make 4 corner setting triangles.

From bright print, cut:

• 128 Bs for leaves.
• 108 Cs for leaves.
• 10 (¾"-wide) strips for outer piping.

From purple print, cut:

• 16 As for large centers.
• 9 Es for small centers.

From dark green print, cut:

• 36 Hs for flower bases.
• 48 Bs for leaves.
• 10 (2¼"-wide) strips for binding.
• 10 (1"-wide) strips for inner piping.

From red/orange print, cut:

• 36 Gs for flowers.

From red print, cut:

• 396 Fs for berries.

From green batik, cut:

• 36 Ds for stems.

Block 1 Assembly

1. Fold and press 1 (17") square as shown in *Appliqué Placement Diagram* to make guidelines for appliqué.

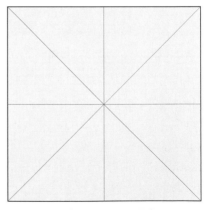

Appliqué Placement Diagram

2. Referring to *Block 1 Diagram*, place and appliqué in order: 8 Cs, 4 Ds, 1 E, 44 Fs, 4 Gs, and 4 Hs.

3. Make 9 of Block 1.

Block 1 Diagram

Block 2 Assembly

1. Fold and press 1 (17") square as shown in *Appliqué Placement Diagram* to make guidelines for appliqué.

2. Referring to *Block 2 Diagram*, place and appliqué in order: 1 A, 8 bright print Bs, and 4 green print Bs.

3. Make 4 of Block 2.

Block 2 Diagram

Quilt Assembly

1. Lay out blocks and setting triangles as shown in *Quilt Top Assembly Diagram*. Join into diagonal rows; join rows to make quilt center.

2. Center 1 border strip on each side of quilt and join. Miter corners.

3. Referring to photo, appliqué bright print flowers as shown on border seam lines. Each flower has 1 A and 8 bright print Bs. Green print Bs are on each side of each flower and in setting triangles. On the seam line between flowers, appliqué 3 bright print Cs. Total appliqué for borders: 12 As, 96 bright print Bs, 32 green print Bs, and 36 bright print Cs.

Quilting and Finishing

1. Divide backing fabric into 3 (2⅝-yard) lengths. Cut 1 piece in half lengthwise. Sew 1 narrow panel between wide panels. Press seam allowances toward narrow panel. Remaining panel is extra and may be used to make a hanging sleeve.

2. Layer backing, batting, and quilt top; baste. Quilt as desired. Quilt shown is ⅛" echo-quilted around appliqué, with flower detail quilted into G and H pieces.

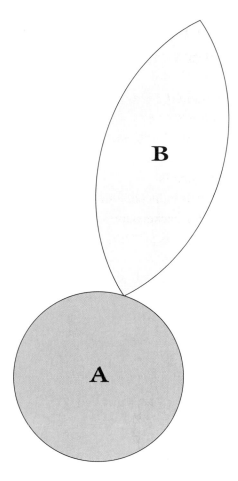

Quilt Top Assembly Diagram

3. Join bright print piping strips into 1 continuous strip. Fold in half lengthwise, right side out, and insert string for piping into fold. Stitch to secure. Repeat with dark green piping strips.

4. Join 2¼"-wide dark green print strips into 1 continuous piece for straight-grain French-fold binding. Press binding in half.

5. Referring to *Binding Assembly Diagrams,* stack dark green piping, bright piping, and dark green binding. Baste together *(Diagram A).*

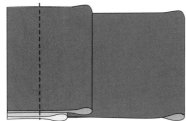

Binding Assembly Diagram A

Attach binding unit to quilt—raw edges of binding even with raw edges of quilt, piping side down—as shown in *Diagram B.* After

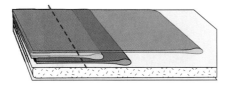

Binding Assembly Diagram B

binding is secured around the quilt, fold top green binding over to encase raw edges of quilt *(Diagram C).* When binding is turned to back, piping will be revealed on front of quilt. Hand-stitch binding to back of quilt.

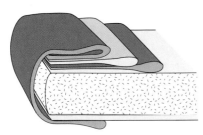

Binding Assembly Diagram C

Freezer-Paper Appliqué

1. Make a freezer-paper template for each piece to be appliquéd. Cut out the templates finished size; you will add seam allowances when you cut out the fabric pieces.

2. Pin the freezer-paper template, shiny side up, to the wrong side of the fabric. Following the template and adding a scant ¼" seam allowance, cut out the fabric piece. Do not remove pins.

3. Using just the tip of a dry iron, press the seam allowance to the shiny side of the paper. Be careful not to touch the freezer paper with the iron.

4. Sharp points, like those used in the petals of this quilt, require special attention. Turn the point down and press it *(Diagram A).* Fold the seam allowance on one side over the point and press it *(Diagram B).* Then, fold the other seam allowance over the point and press *(Diagram C).*

Diagram A   *Diagram B*   *Diagram C*

5. When pressing curved edges, like the red flowers in this quilt, clip sharp inward curves *(Diagram D).* If the shape doesn't curve smoothy, separate the paper from the fabric with your fingernail and try again.

Diagram D

6. Remove the pins when all seam allowances have been pressed to the freezer paper. Position the prepared appliqué right side up on the background fabric. Press to adhere it to the background fabric. A large appliqué should also be pinned in place to make it secure.

7. After appliquéing in place, trim the fabric from behind the shape, leaving seam allowances in place. Separate the freezer paper from the fabric with your fingernail and pull gently to remove it. Or, if you prefer not to trim the background fabric, pull out the freezer paper before you complete stitching around the appliqué.

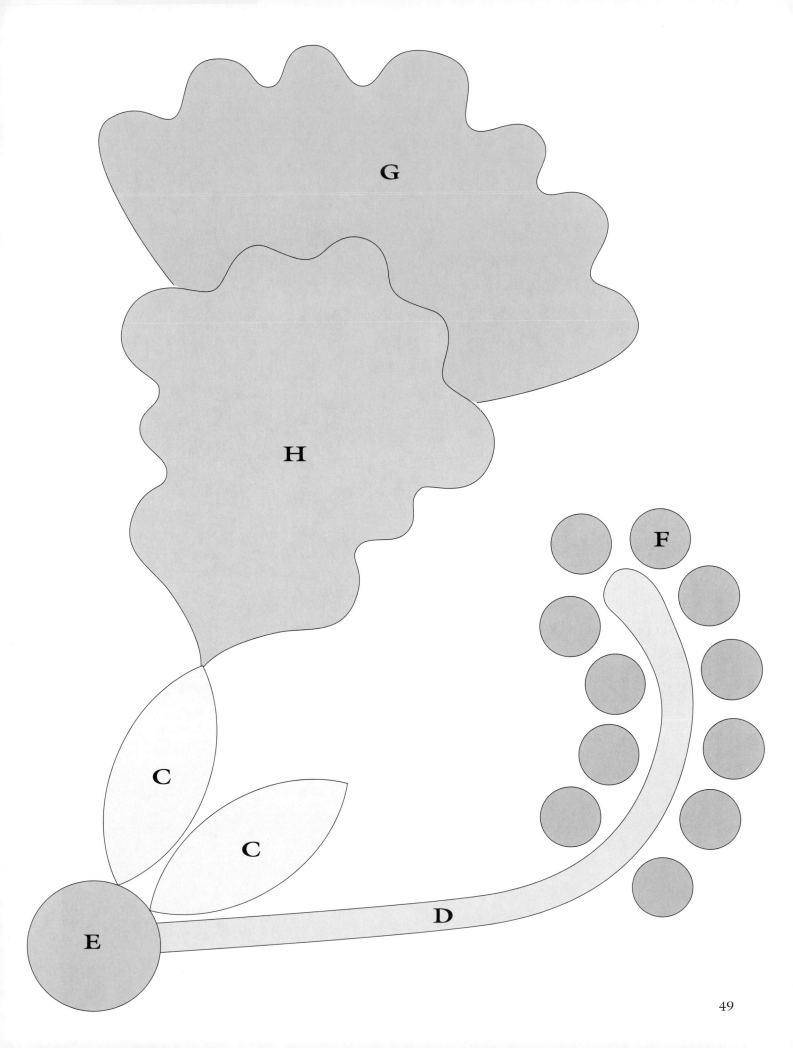

Connie Brown
Asheville, North Carolina

Connie Brown, along with her husband and son, moved from their hometown of Memphis, Tennessee to Asheville, North Carolina, in 1989. Connie was experienced in all types of crafts, but had never quilted. After the move, she saw a class listing for a beginning quilt class at the local community college. She signed up and has been quilting ever since. "The teacher, Mary Field, was wonderful," Connie recalls. "I learned so much from Mary—all the basics. To this day, I refer back to those class notes."

Shortly after taking the class in 1990, Connie joined the Asheville Quilt

"Color is my inspiration. I find that I am drawn to an object because of a color."

Guild and took many workshops. She has held several offices in her guild, including president, vice president, ways and means chairperson, and served twice as the quilt show chairperson. She has been the curator for many of her guild's special exhibits, including festival displays, museum and gallery exhibits, and even a display at the Biltmore Estate.

"Color is my inspiration," says Connie. "I find that I am drawn to an object because of a color. I'll figure out which color pulled me in and then look to see which colors are around it and how they affect each other."

Connie's work has been juried into major quilt shows throughout the country. She's won a total of nine 1st place, nine 2nd place, three 3rd place, three honorable mentions, and three best of show ribbons. She even won a grand prize for her machine quilting—a new Bernina!

Target
2001

Connie Brown wanted to make a quilt with many red fabrics, but had no actual design or plan in mind. "A television commercial that featured red packaged products was the inspiration I needed," she says.

To keep the reds warm and hot, Connie chose a complementary green with yellow undertones. "I went to my stash and started pulling out fabrics I felt would work," she says.

Connie enjoys working with curves, and she started randomly pairing up fabrics and making Drunkard's Path units—not matching fabrics, but using whatever was next in the stacks. "After I had about 100 units made, I took them to the design wall and positioned them until I had a pleasing design."

In 2002, *Target* was juried into the American Quilter's Society Show, the Quilter's Heritage Celebration, the International Quilt Festival, and the Mid-Atlantic Quilt Festival, where it won Honorable Mention. It also appeared in the December 2002 edition of *Quilter's Newsletter Magazine*.

Target

Finished Size

Quilt: 72"x 84"

Blocks: 30 (11⅝") Target Blocks

Materials

4 yards assorted light prints in whites, yellows, and greens for blocks

4 yards assorted dark prints in reds and greens for blocks

3 yards assorted red prints from medium to dark for border

⅝ yard red solid for sashing

⅜ yard green print for piping

¾ yard print for binding

5 yards fabric for backing

Twin-size batting

Cutting

Instructions are for rotary cutting and quick piecing. Cut pieces in order listed to make best use of yardage. Patterns are on pages 54–55.

From assorted light prints, cut:

- 60 As.
- 60 Bs.
- 60 Cs.
- 40 (2½") squares for appliqué.

From assorted dark prints, cut:

- 60 As.
- 60 Bs.
- 60 Cs.
- 40 (2½") squares for appliqué.

From red prints, cut:

- 48 As.
- 48 Bs.
- 48 Cs.

From solid red, cut:

- 17 (1"-wide) strips. Piece strips to make 5 (1" x 60⅝") horizontal sashing strips. Cut remaining strips into 24 (1" x 12⅛") vertical sashing strips.

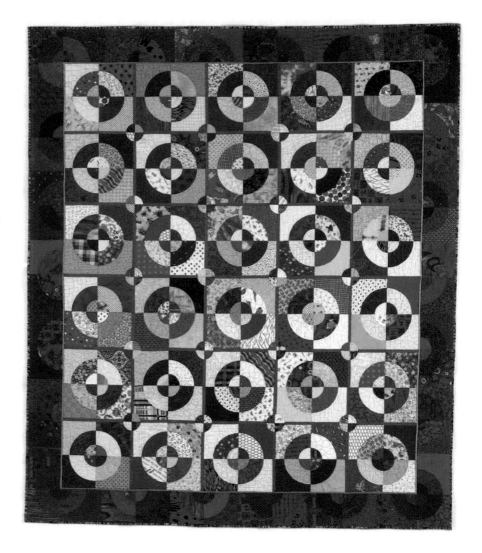

From green print, cut:

- 8 (1"-wide) strips. Join to make 2 (1" x 72¾") side strips and 2 (1" x 60⅝") top and bottom strips. Fold in half lengthwise, right side out, for piping strips.

From binding fabric, cut:

- 9 (2¼"-wide) strips for binding.

Block Assembly

1. Choose 1 light A, 1 dark B and 1 light C. Join as shown in *Light Quarter Block Assembly Diagram*

Light Quarter Block Assembly Diagram

to make 1 light quarter block. Repeat.

2. Choose 1 dark A, 1 light B and 1 dark C. Join as shown *Dark Quarter Block Assembly Diagram* to make 1 dark quarter block. Repeat.

Dark Quarter Block Assembly Diagram

3. Lay out 2 light and 2 dark quarter blocks as shown in *Block Assembly Diagram*. Join. Trim block evenly to 12⅛" square to make 1 Target block.

4. Make 30 Target blocks.

5. To make border units, choose 1 each red A, B, and C. Join as shown in *Block Assembly Diagram* above to make 1 border unit. Make 48 border units.

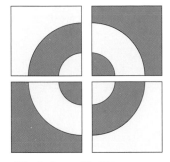

Block Assembly Diagram

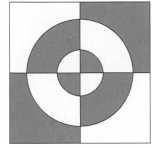

Block Diagram

Quilt Assembly

1. Referring to *Quilt Top Assembly Diagram*, lay out blocks and vertical sashing strips, rotating blocks as shown. Join to make 1 block row. Make 6 block rows.

2. Alternate block rows with horizontal sashing strips and join.

3. Referring to *Sashing Unit Assembly Diagram*, join 2 dark and 2 light 2½" squares to make a Four-Patch unit. Press. Center circle template D on square and cut out. Repeat to make 20 circles.

Sashing Unit Assembly Diagram

Appliqué pieced circles on sashing intersections to complete center.

4. Position piping strips at top and bottom of quilt. Baste in place. Repeat for side piping strips.

5. Join 12 border units as shown to make 1 side border. Repeat. Check borders for fit and adjust seams if needed. Add borders to quilt. (Piping will be sandwiched between the quilt top and borders.)

6. Join 12 border units as shown to make top border. Repeat for bottom border. Check borders for fit and adjust seams if needed. Add borders to quilt. (Piping will be sandwiched between the quilt top and borders.)

Quilting and Finishing

1. Divide backing fabric into 2 (2½-yard) lengths. Cut 1 piece in half lengthwise. Sew 1 narrow panel to each side of wide panel. Press seam allowances toward narrow panels.

2. Layer backing, batting, and quilt top; baste. Quilt as desired. Quilt shown is machine-quilted in geometric patterns and loops.

3. Join 2¼"-wide binding strips into 1 continuous piece for straight-grain French-fold binding. Add binding to quilt.

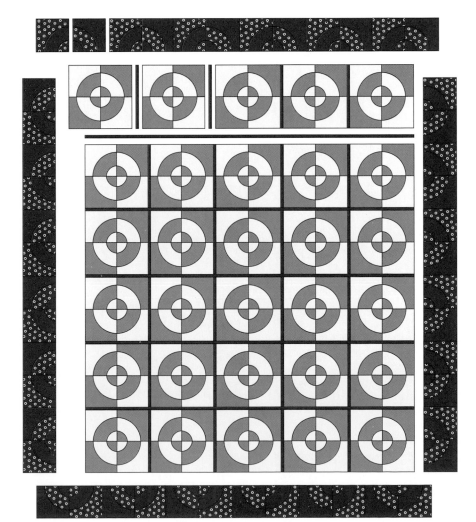

Quilt Top Assembly Diagram

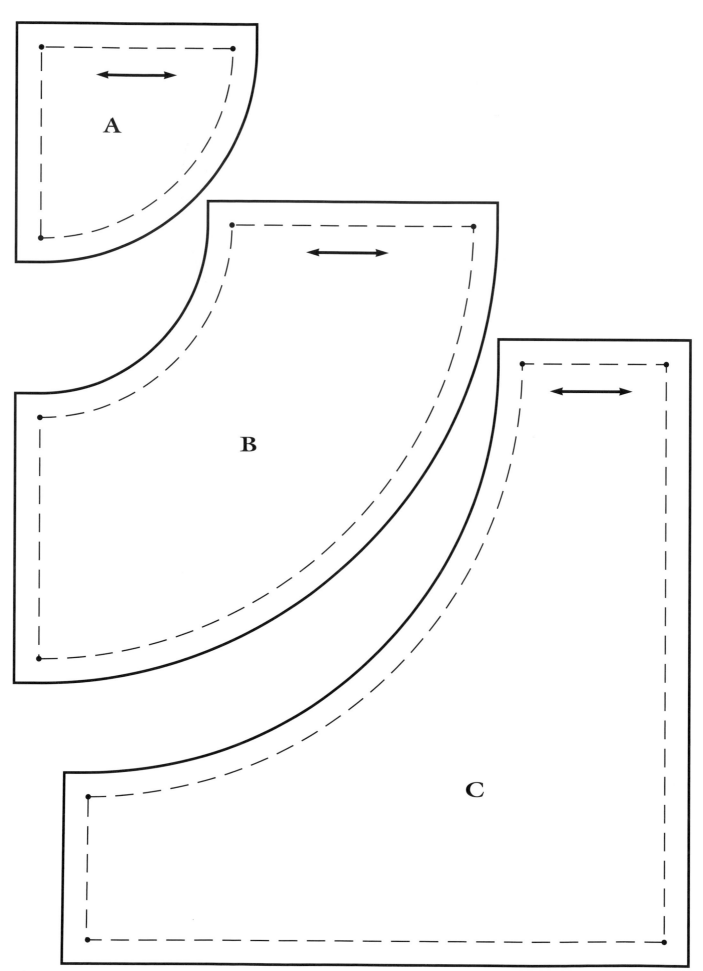

A

B

C

54

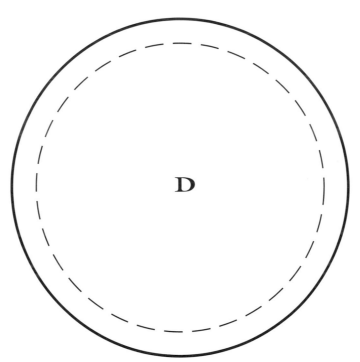

D

Chartreuse Targét

Finished Size
Quilt: 72"x 84"

Connie Brown made another quilt from her *Target* pattern. This one is pronounced with the faux French accent, *tar 'jay*.

"I enjoyed working on the red *Target* so much," says Connie. "There was no planning or worrying over matching fabrics. I just gathered a bunch of fabrics in the same family, cut them up, and sewed."

While trying to decide what to do for her next quilt, Connie took a long look at her fabric stash. "I realized that I had a lot of sour apple, chartreuse, and poison green fabrics," she says. "I thought this would be a good color scheme for another version of the same quilt."

Just as with the red version, Connie stacked up the greens (both lights and darks), light fabrics, and a few wild prints. She randomly paired them and made units.

"The main difference in the construction of these two quilts is the border," says Connie. "The reds worked well in a color-on-color pieced border, but the greens did not make the same subtle statement. So I opted to use just squares of fabric for this border."

55

Barbara Clem
Dublin, Ohio

$\mathcal{B}$arbara Clem began quilting in 1984 when she quit working outside the home to raise her two sons, Jonathan and Jacob. "My mother-in-law, Ruth Clem, felt that I needed a hobby, and remembered my admiring a Log Cabin quilt in a fabric shop window years ago," Barbara recalls. "My husband Lyle traveled a lot, so when Ruth sent me a box of fabric and pattern for the Log Cabin quilt, I set to work. Fortunately, my mother taught me how to sew while I was growing up, so converting to quiltmaking came easily for me."

Barbara had shown horses and dogs in her youth, so entering her quilts into competitions was a logical next step for her. She began at the local level and quickly progressed to national and international shows. "Each quilt and competition is a learning experience," Barbara says. "Each time that I felt I had reached a plateau, I surpassed my expectations and soared to new heights. There is so much to learn and so much fun in the learning and sharing."

"When the top is going together, you get excited because it's so pretty. When you quilt, it's the icing on the cake."

As Barbara's quilting skills progressed, she learned to hand quilt. "I remember my first one, knowing that once I started it by hand, I would finish it by hand," says Barbara. "I remember saying, 'never again!' But that 'never' just lasted until my next quilt."

Barbara enjoys every step of the quiltmaking process. "When the top is going together, you get excited because it's so pretty. When you quilt, it's the icing on the cake."

Calico Rose
2001

Calico Rose is a variation of a very old design called Rose of 1840. Barbara Clem confesses to not having much patience for snowflake cutting; so her friend Jan Halgrimson drew the basic bud designs, and Barbara took things from there.

Calico Rose *has been exhibited at the following shows:*

• 1st Place Wall Hanging, Best in Show, Best Binding, and Best Hand Quilting at the 2001 Kaleidoscope of Quilts X in Toledo, Ohio
• Exhibited at the National Quilt Association Show in Tulsa, Oklahoma
• Exhibited at the 2001 World Quilt and Textile Show

• Juried into the 2002 International Quilt Festival in Houston, Texas and shown on the Bernina Web site
• Juried into the 2002 Mid-Atlantic Quilt Festival
• Exhibited at the 2002 Minnesota Quilt Show
• 1st Place and Best in Show at the 2002 Ohio State Fair

Calico Rose

Finished Size

Quilt: 72½" x 72½"

Blocks: 5 (17½") Calico Rose Blocks

Materials

3½ yards white-on-cream lace print for background and appliqué

4 yards tan for block backgrounds

¾ yard red print #1 for appliqué

⅜ yard red print #2 for appliqué

1½ yards green print #1 for stems

2 yards green print #2 for appliqué and binding

½ yard gold print for appliqué

5½ yards fabric for backing

Full-size batting

Additional batting or trapunto yarn for stuffwork

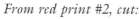

Cutting

Instructions are for rotary cutting and quick piecing. Cut pieces in order listed to make best use of yardage. Patterns are on pages 60–61.

From white-on-cream lace print, cut:

- 4 (19") squares for appliqué background blocks.
- 8 (2½"-wide) strips. Join strips to make 4 (2½" x 81") outer border strips.
- 50" of 1½"-wide bias strip. Fold and press into thirds. Cut into 4 (3½"-long) A stems and 4 (6½"-long) side triangle stems.
- 75" of 1⅛"-wide bias strip. Fold and press into thirds. Cut into 8 (5"-long) B stems and 4 (7"-long) corner triangle stems.
- 1 C.
- 1 E.
- 8 Gs.

- 20 Hs.
- 12 Is.
- 12 Js.
- 8 Ks.
- 8 Ms.
- 164 Ns.
- 8 Os.

From tan, cut:

- 2¼ yards. Cut yardage into 4 (10"-wide) lengthwise strips for border.
- 1 (19") center square.
- 1 (26½") square. Cut square in quarters diagonally to make 4 side setting triangles.
- 2 (13½") squares. Cut squares in half diagonally to make 4 corner setting triangles.
- 1 D.
- 1 F.

From red print #1, cut:

- 8 Cs.
- 36 Ks.

From red print #2, cut:

- 8 Es.
- 24 Is.

From green print #1, cut:

- 60" of 1½"-wide bias strip. Fold and press into thirds. Cut into 16 (3½"-long) A stems.
- 275" of 1⅛"-wide bias strip. Fold and press into thirds. Cut into 24 (5"-long) B stems, 4 (10"-long) border stems, and 8 (13"-long) corner border stems.

From green print #2, cut:

- 56 Gs.
- 64 Hs.
- 24 Js.
- 36 Ms.
- 1 yard for bias binding.

From gold print, cut:

- 8 Ds.
- 8 Fs.
- 36 Ls.

Block Assembly

Note: All appliqué (except white arcs) is stuffed, either with additional batting or trapunto yarn. In addition, detail is quilted into all flower units before quilt is layered.

1. For colored appliqué blocks, fold 1 (19") white-on-cream square in quarters horizontally and vertically as shown in *Folding Diagram*. Press to make appliqué guidelines.

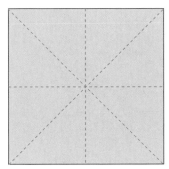

Folding Diagram

2. Referring to *Appliqué Placement Diagram*, position 4 A stems and 4 B stems. Tuck 1 H leaf under each stem as shown. Appliqué. Add 8 G leaves.

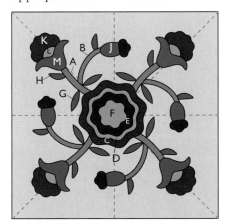

Appliqué Placement Diagram

3. Stack and appliqué 1 each C, D, E, and F as a separate rose unit. Position rose unit. Join 1 each I and J as a separate bud unit. Repeat to make 4 bud units. Position on block. Stack and appliqué 1 each K, L, and M to make 1 flower unit.

Repeat to make 4 flower units. Position on block.

4. Appliqué units in place, stuffing with additional batting. Quilt detail into interior of each unit. Trim block evenly to 18" square to complete 1 colored appliqué block.

5. Make 4 colored appliqué blocks.

6. For center block, press guidelines into tan square as in Step 1. Proceed as in colored appliqué block, omitting L piece in flower units. (The K and M pieces may be appliquéd separately, rather than as a unit.) Trim block to 18" square. Appliqué 6 N arcs to each side of block to complete.

7. To make side setting triangles, position 1 A stem and 1 B stem as shown. Add 1 H leaf to each stem and appliqué pieces. Add 1 each I, J, K, and M. Add 12 N arcs to

short sides of triangle as shown to complete. Make 4 appliquéd side setting triangles.

8. To make corner triangles, position and appliqué 1 B stem, 1 H, 1 I, and 1 J as shown. Appliqué 6 N arcs on long side of triangle to complete. Make 4 appliquéd corner triangles.

9. For borders, join 1 white-on-cream strip to 1 long edge of each tan strip to make 4 border strips. Borders will be centered on quilt with corners mitered.

10. Appliqué 17 N arc units to inner tan edge of each border.

11. On center of each border, appliqué 1 (10"-long) stem, 2 H leaves, and 3 K/L/M flower units. Stuff and quilt detail into flower units.

12. On one end of border, position and appliqué 1 (10"-long)

Quilt Top Assembly Diagram

stem, 3 H leaves, 1 I J bud unit, and 1 K/L/M flower unit. (Corner end of stem will be covered by a corner rose.) Stuff and quilt detail into both flower units. Repeat for both ends of each border as shown.

Quilt Assembly

1. Lay out center block, 4 color blocks, and setting triangles, trimming to fit. Join into diagonal rows; join rows to complete quilt center.

2. Add borders to quilt, mitering corners.

3. Stack and appliqué 1 each C, D, E, and F to make 1 corner rose. Make 4 corner roses. Stuff and appliqué in place, covering stem ends. Quilt interior detail of rose. Add 6 G leaves to each corner. Add 2 O leaves to each corner.

Quilting and Finishing

1. Divide backing fabric into 2 (2¼-yard) lengths. Cut 1 piece in half lengthwise. Sew 1 narrow panel to each side of wide panel. Press seam allowances toward narrow panels.

2. Layer backing, batting, and quilt top; baste. Quilt as desired. Quilt shown is outline-quilted around appliqué. Color blocks are filled with echo quilting. Center block is filled with a cathedral window pattern, side triangles are filled with a broken six pointed star pattern, and corner triangles are filled with a hexagonal basket weave pattern. Borders feature wreath and swag patterns around appliqué with diagonal fill.

3. Make 11 yards of 2¼"-wide bias binding. Mark scallops on quilt border as shown. Add binding to quilt, trimming excess border before turning binding to back of quilt.

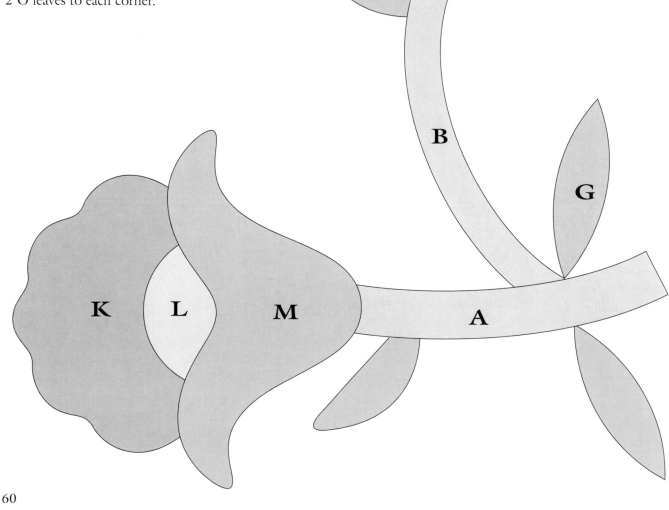

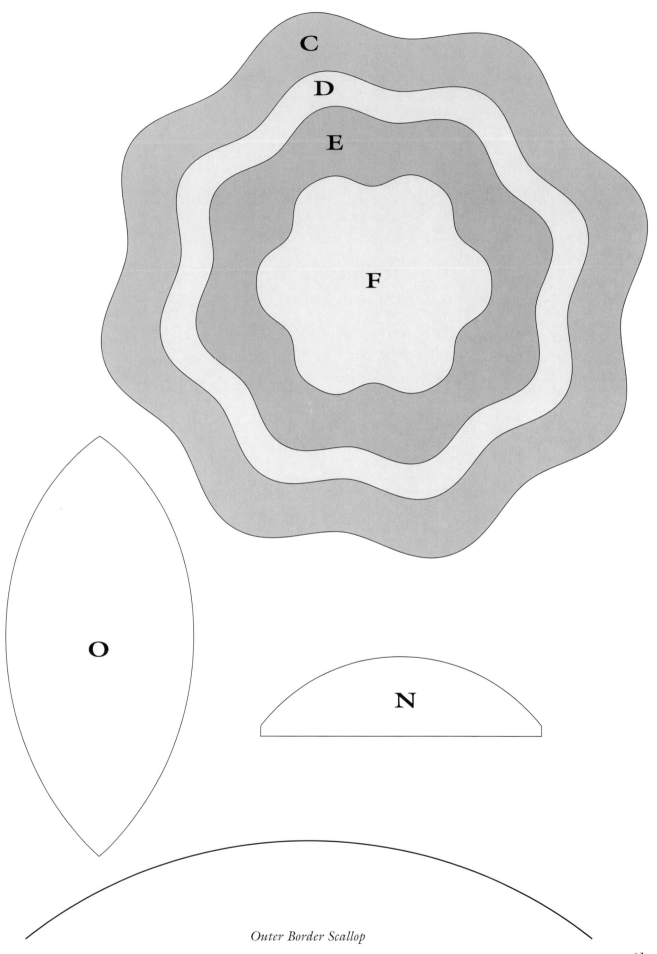

Outer Border Scallop

Scott A. Murkin
Asheboro, North Carolina

Dr. Scott Murkin began quilting in 1994, when he decided that his two-year-old daughter needed a quilt. "I had seen my grandma, aunt, and great aunt make quilts and even helped them cut out patterns. So I figured I knew how," says Scott. "I figured wrong, but fortunately, I didn't let that stop me. I have never taken a quilting class, but I have a quilting library of over 500 volumes that has taught me much. Experience has done the rest. I joined the Randolph Quilter's Guild in 1997 and began exhibiting the next year, opening up a whole new world of delight for me and my family."

Although Scott is a medical doctor by profession, he still finds time to quilt every day. He describes himself as a dabbler who loves both traditional and contemporary designs. All of his quilts are originals, or original variations of traditional blocks. "I use both hand and machine techniques, and I rarely do the same thing twice," he says. "I believe variety is the spice of life."

"I have a quilting library of over 500 volumes that has taught me much. Experience has done the rest."

In addition to teaching programs and workshops at regional quilt shops and quilt guilds, Scott also appraises antique quilts and judges quilt shows. "All aspects of quilts and quiltmaking fascinate me," he says.

Cherokee Heritage
2001

Cherokee Heritage was a finalist and part of *Quilter's Newsletter Magazine's* traveling exhibit, "Reflections of Heritage," which appeared in Barcelona, Spain; Houston, Texas; and other cities.

"My great-great-grandmother was a Cherokee who married off the reservation and integrated with non-Native Americans," Scott explains. "The Cherokee never developed significant needle arts, so I integrated traditional basket-weaving patterns into the patchwork and quilting motifs.

"Many Native Americans used a four-color palette in their decorative arts as a spiritual symbol of the four elements of nature, the four cardinal points of the compass, and the four races of man. Red, yellow, black, and white were used most often, but sometimes, blue was substituted for yellow.

"There is a clarity to the central design, representing the core Cherokee values and beliefs. There is a parallel clarity in the border design, representing a strong front that was presented to the outside world. In between, there is a struggle between balance and chaos, resulting in some disharmony. This disharmony represents the historic Cherokee struggle."

Cherokee Heritage

Finished Size
Quilt: 76¼" x 76½"

Materials
Refer to photo and to *Quilt Top Assembly Diagram* when selecting fabrics for this quilt.

8 red prints:
- ½ yard (#1)
- 1 fat eighth (9" x 22") (#2)
- 1 fat eighth (9" x 22") (#3)
- ¾ yard (#4)
- ⅜ yard (#5)
- ⅜ yard (#6)
- ½ yard (#7)
- ¼ yard (#8)

8 white prints:
- 1 (5½") square (#1)
- 1 fat eighth (9" x 22") (#2)
- ¼ yard (#3)
- 1 fat quarter (18" x 22") (#4)
- 1 fat eighth (9" x 22") (#5)
- ⅜ yard (#6)
- 1¼ yards (#7)
- ⅜ yard (#8)
- ½ yard black-and-white stripe

12 black prints:
- 1 fat eighth (9" x 22") (#1)
- 1 fat eighth (9" x 22") (#2)
- ⅜ yard (#3)
- ½ yard (#4)
- ½ yard (#5)
- ½ yard (#6)
- ⅜ yard (#7)
- ⅝ yard (#8)
- 1 fat eighth (9" x 22") (#9)
- ¾ yard (#10)
- ⅝ yard (#11)
- ¾ yard (#12)
- ¾ yard blue print

4¾ yards fabric for backing

Full-size batting

Cutting
Instructions are for rotary cutting and quick piecing. Cut pieces in order listed to make best use of yardage. Units are numbered from the center out. We suggest placing units in labeled zip-top bags as you cut to keep pieces organized.

From red #1, cut:
- 2 (4⅜") squares. Cut squares in half diagonally to make 4 triangles for Block 1.
- 8 (1½"-wide) strips. Piece strips to make 2 (1½" x 74¾") top and bottom borders and 2 (1½" x 76¾") side borders. (Border strips are exact length needed. You may want to cut them longer to allow for piecing variations.)

From red #2, cut:
- 2 (2¼" x 16½") strips for Strip 2.

From red #3, cut:
- 4 (4⅜") squares. Cut squares in half diagonally to make 8 triangles for Block 4.

From red #4, cut:
- 2 (4⅜") squares. Cut squares in half diagonally to make 4 triangles for Block 7.
- 6 (2¼" x 16½") strips for Strip 5.
- 2 (2¼" x 16½") strips for Strip 9.
- 4 (2¼" x 16½") strips for Strip 10.
- 2 (2¼" x 16½") strips for Strip 15.

From red #5, cut:
- 4 (4⅜") squares. Cut squares in half diagonally to make 8 triangles for Block 8.
- 4 (4⅜") squares. Cut squares in half diagonally to make 8 triangles for Block 13.
- 4 (4⅜") squares. Cut squares in half diagonally to make 8 triangles for Block 14.
- 4 (4⅜") squares. Cut squares in half diagonally to make 8 trian-

gles for Block 20.

From red #6, cut:

- 2 ($2\frac{1}{4}$" x $16\frac{1}{2}$") strips for Strip 9.
- 2 ($2\frac{1}{4}$" x $16\frac{1}{2}$") strips for Strip 11.
- 2 ($2\frac{1}{4}$" x $16\frac{1}{2}$") strips for Strip 16.
- 2 ($2\frac{1}{4}$" x $16\frac{1}{2}$") strips for Strip 17.

From red #7, cut:

- 6 (2"-wide) strips for Border Strip 23.

From red #8, cut:

- 16 ($2\frac{5}{8}$") squares. Cut squares in half diagonally to make 32 small triangles for Edge Unit 24.
- 14 ($2\frac{5}{8}$") squares. Cut squares in half diagonally to make 28 small triangles for Fill Unit 25.

From white #1, cut:

- 1 ($5\frac{1}{2}$") square for Block 1.

From white #2, cut:

- 1 (4" x $16\frac{1}{2}$") strip for Strip 2.

From white #3, cut:

- 4 ($5\frac{1}{2}$") squares for Block 4.

From white #4, cut:

- 3 (4" x $16\frac{1}{2}$") strips for Strip 5.

From white #5, cut:

- 2 (1" x $16\frac{1}{2}$") strips for Strip 15.
- 2 (1" x $16\frac{1}{2}$") strips for Strip 16.

From white #6, cut:

- 16 (4") squares for Square 19.

From white #7, cut:

- 12 ($2\frac{5}{8}$") squares. Cut squares in half diagonally to make 24 small triangles for Block 20.
- 6 ($2\frac{5}{8}$") squares. Cut squares in half diagonally to make 12 small triangles for Block 21.
- 12 ($2\frac{5}{8}$") squares. Cut squares in half diagonally to make 24 small triangles for Block 22.
- 12 ($1\frac{1}{2}$"-wide) strips for Border Strip 23.
- 8 ($1\frac{1}{2}$"-wide) strips. Cut strips into 72 ($1\frac{1}{2}$" x 4") rectangles for Border Strip 23.

From white #8, cut:

- 16 (4") squares for Edge Unit 24.

From black-and-white stripe, cut:

- 4 ($5\frac{1}{2}$") squares for Block 7.
- 4 (6") squares. Cut 2 squares in half diagonally from upper right to lower left and cut 2 squares in half diagonally from upper left to lower right to make 8 triangles for Block 8. You may want to make the squares over-sized to allow for matching stripes in the block center. If so, trim joined triangles to $5\frac{1}{2}$" square when completed.

From black #1, cut:

- 4 (4") squares for Square 3.

From black #2, cut:

- 4 ($4\frac{3}{8}$") squares. Cut squares in half diagonally to make 8 triangles for Block 4.

From black #3, cut:

- 8 (4") squares for Square 6.
- 6 ($4\frac{3}{8}$") squares. Cut squares in half diagonally to make 12 triangles for Block 7.
- 4 ($4\frac{3}{8}$") squares. Cut squares in half diagonally to make 8 triangles for Block 8.

From black #4, cut:

- 2 (4" x $16\frac{1}{2}$") strips for Strip 9.
- 2 (4" x $16\frac{1}{2}$") strips for Strip 10.
- 1 (4" x $16\frac{1}{2}$") strip for Strip 11.

From black #5, cut:

- 12 (4") squares for Square 12.
- 8 ($4\frac{3}{8}$") squares. Cut squares in half diagonally to make 16 triangles for Block 14.

From black #6, cut:

- 4 ($5\frac{1}{2}$") squares for Block 13.
- 8 ($5\frac{1}{2}$") squares for Block 14.

From black #7, cut:

- 4 ($4\frac{3}{8}$") squares. Cut squares in half diagonally to make 8 triangles for Block 13.
- 4 ($4\frac{3}{8}$") squares. Cut squares in half diagonally to make 8 triangles for Block 14.
- 2 ($4\frac{3}{8}$") squares. Cut squares in

half diagonally to make 4 triangles for Block 21.

From black #8, cut:

- 2 (4" x $16\frac{1}{2}$") strips for Strip 15.
- 2 (4" x $16\frac{1}{2}$") strips for Strip 16.
- 2 (4" x $16\frac{1}{2}$") strips for Strip 17.
- 1 (4" x $16\frac{1}{2}$") strip for Strip 18.

From black #9, cut:

- 2 (1" x $16\frac{1}{2}$") strips for Strip 17.
- 2 (1" x $16\frac{1}{2}$") strips for Strip 18.

From black #10, cut:

- 8 ($5\frac{1}{2}$") squares for Block 20.
- 4 ($5\frac{1}{2}$") squares for Block 21.
- 4 ($5\frac{1}{2}$") squares for Block 22.
- 4 ($2\frac{5}{8}$") squares. Cut squares in half diagonally to make 8 small triangles for Block 20.
- 2 ($2\frac{5}{8}$") squares. Cut squares in half diagonally to make 4 small triangles for Block 21.
- 4 ($2\frac{5}{8}$") squares. Cut squares in half diagonally to make 8 small triangles for Block 22.

From black #11, cut:

- 48 ($2\frac{5}{8}$") squares. Cut squares in half diagonally to make 96 small triangles for Edge Unit 24.
- 42 ($2\frac{5}{8}$") squares. Cut squares in half diagonally to make 84 small triangles for Fill Unit 25.

From black #12, cut:

- 9 ($2\frac{1}{4}$"-wide) strips for binding.

From blue, cut:

- 4 ($1\frac{1}{8}$" x $16\frac{1}{2}$") strips for Strip 15.
- 4 ($1\frac{1}{8}$" x $16\frac{1}{2}$") strips for Strip 16.
- 4 ($1\frac{1}{8}$" x $16\frac{1}{2}$") strips for Strip 17.
- 4 ($1\frac{1}{8}$" x $16\frac{1}{2}$") strips for Strip 18.
- 8 ($4\frac{3}{8}$") squares. Cut squares in half diagonally to make 16 triangles for Block 20.
- 4 ($4\frac{3}{8}$") squares. Cut squares in half diagonally to make 8 triangles for Block 21.
- 4 ($4\frac{3}{8}$") squares. Cut squares in half diagonally to make 8 triangles for Block 22.

General Block and Strip Assembly

1. Position or label units as each is completed.

2. For blocks, choose 1 center square and 4 triangles as indicated. Join 1 triangle to each side, working in opposite pairs, to complete 1 block. For outer blocks, assemble 1 (4-triangle) unit as shown and substitute for 1 large triangle. Other variations are listed with individual units.

3. For strips, assemble strip sets as indicated. Cut strip set into segments to make strips.

Units

1. To make *Block 1*, use 1 white #1 center and 4 red #1 triangles. Join to make 1 center block.

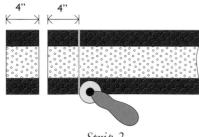

Block 1

2. To make *Strip 2*, join 1 (2¼" x 16½") red #2 strip to each long side of 1 (4" x 16½") white #2 strip to make 1 strip set.

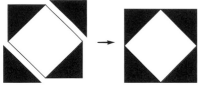

Strip 2

Cut strip set into 4 (4"-wide) segments for Strip 2. *Square 3* was prepared under Cutting.

Square 3

3. To make *Block 4*, use 1 white #3 center, 2 red #3 triangles, and 2 black #2 triangles. Join as shown to make 1 of Block 4. Make 4 of Block 4.

Block 4

4. To make *Strip 5*, join 1 (2¼" x 16½") red #4 strips to each long side of 1 (4" x 16½") white #4 strip to make 1 strip set. Make 3 strip sets. Cut strip sets into 12 (4"-wide) segments for Strip 5. *Square 6* was prepared under Cutting.

Strip 5

Square 6

5. To make *Block 7*, use 1 stripe center, 1 red #4 triangle, and 3 black #2 triangles. Join as shown to make 1 of Block 7. Make 4 of Block 7, placing red triangle as shown.

Block 7

6. To make *Block 8*, join 2 stripe triangles, matching stripes, to make

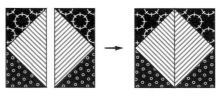

Block 8

center square. Add 2 red #5 and 2 black #3 triangles to complete 1 Block 8. Make 4 of Block 8.

7. To make *Strip 9*, join 1 (2¼" x 16½") red #4 strip, 1 (4" x 16½") black #4 strip, and 1 (2¼" x 16½") red #6 strip to make 1 strip set. Make 2 strip sets. Cut strip sets into 8 (4"-wide) segments for Strip 9.

Strip 9

8. To make *Strip 10*, join 1 (2¼" x 16½") red #4 strip to each long side of 1 (4" x 16½") black #4 strip to make 1 strip set. Make 2 strip sets. Cut strip sets into 8 (4"-wide) segments for Strip 10.

Strip 10

9. To make *Strip 11*, join 1 (2¼" x 16½") red #6 strip to each long side of 1 (4" x 16½") black #4 strip to make 1 strip set. Cut strip set into 4 (4"-wide) segments for Strip 11. *Square 12* was prepared under Cutting.

Strip 11

Square 12

10. To make *Block 13*, use 1 black #6 center, 2 red #5 triangles, and 2 black #7 triangles. Join as shown to make 1 of Block 13.

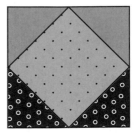

Block 13

Make 4 of Block 13.

11. To make *Block 14*, use 1 black #6 center, 1 red #5 triangle, 1 black #7 triangle, and 2 black #5 triangles. Join as shown to make 1 of Block 14. Make 4 blocks with red on right and 4 blocks with red on left.

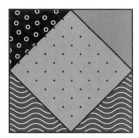

Block 14 Left

Block 14 Right

12. To make *Strip 15*, join 1 (1⅛" x 16½") blue strip to each long side of 1 (1" x 16½") white #5 strip to make top strip. Join to 1 (4" x 16½") black #8 strip. Add 1 (2¼" x 16½") red #4 strip to bottom to make 1 strip set. Make 2 strip sets. Cut strip sets into 8 (4"-wide) segments to make 8 of Strip 15.

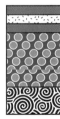

Strip 15

13. To make *Strip 16*, join 1 (1⅛" x 16½") blue strip to each long side of 1 (1" x 16½") white #5 strip to make top strip. Join to 1 (4" x 16½") black

Strip 16

#8 strip. Add 1 (2¼" x 16½") red #6 strip to bottom to make 1 strip set. Make 2 strip sets. Cut strip sets into 8 (4"-wide) segments to make 8 of Strip 16.

14. To make *Strip 17*, join 1 (1⅛" x 16½") blue strip to each long side of 1 (1" x 16½") black #9 strip to make top strip. Join to 1 (4" x 16½") black #8 strip. Add 1 (2¼" x 16½") red #6 strip to bottom to make 1 strip set. Make 2 strip sets. Cut strip sets into 8 (4"-wide) segments to make 8 of Strip 17.

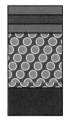

Strip 17

15. To make *Strip 18*, join 1 (1⅛" x 16½") blue strip to each long side of 1 (1" x 16½") black #9 strip to make top strip. Repeat for bottom strip. Join these strips to 1 (4" x 16½") black #8 strip. Cut strip set into 4 (4"-wide) segments to make 4 of Strip 18.

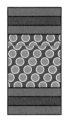

Strip 18

16. *Square 19* was prepared under Cutting.

Square 19

17. To make *Block 20*, use 1 black #10 center, 1 red #5 and 2 blue triangles. Join to make lower portion of block. Join 1 black #10 and 3 white #7 small triangles to

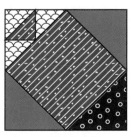

Block 20

make top triangle unit. Add to top to complete 1 of Block 20. Make 8 of Block 20.

18. To make *Block 21*, use 1 black #10 center, 1 black #7 and 2 blue triangles. Join to make lower portion of block. Join 1 black #10 and 3 white #7 small triangles to make top triangle unit. Add to top to complete 1 of Block 21. Make 4 of Block 21.

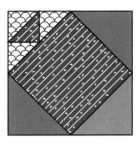

Block 21

19. To make *Block 22*, use 1 black #10 center and 2 blue triangles. Join to make lower half of block. Join 1 black #10 and 3 white #7 small triangles to make top triangle unit. Repeat. Add 2 triangle units to top to complete 1 of Block 22. Make 4 of block 22.

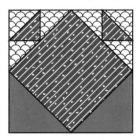

Block 22

20. To make *Border Strip 23*, join 1 (1½"-wide) white #7 strip to each long side of 1 (2"-wide) red #7 strip to make 1 strip set. Make 6 strip sets. Cut strip sets into 36 (5½"-wide) segments. Join 1 (1½" x 4") white #7 rectangle to each end to complete 1 border strip. Make 36 border strips.

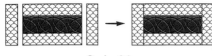

Strip 23

Edge Unit 24

Fill Unit 25

21. To make *Edge Unit 24,* join 1 red #8 and 3 black #11 small triangles to make 1 triangle unit. Make 32 triangle units. Join 2 triangle units to 1 white #8 square as shown to make 1 Edge Unit 24.

Make 16 of Edge Unit 24.

22. To make *Fill Unit 25,* join 1 red #8 and 3 black #11 small triangles to make 1 Fill Unit 25. Make 28 fill units.

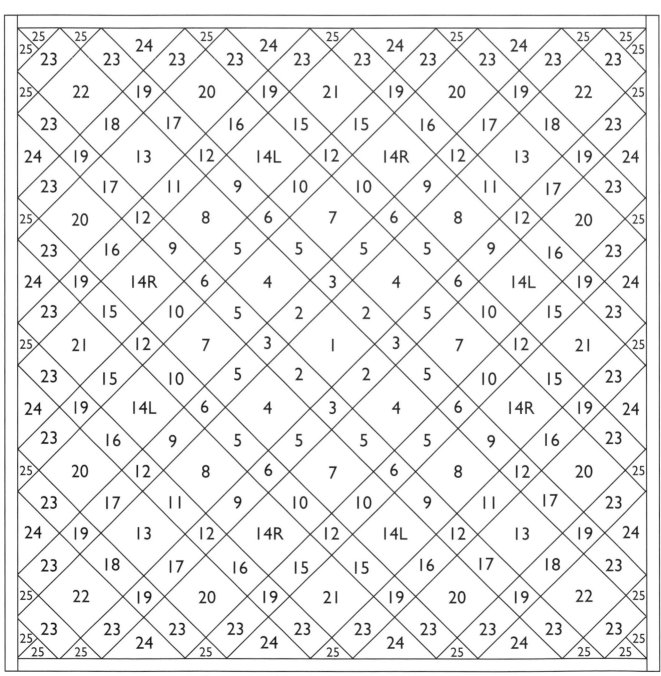

Quilt Top Assembly Diagram (by block/strip number)

Quilt Assembly

Refer carefully to *Quilt Top Assembly Diagram*.
1. Lay out all pieces as shown in *Quilt Top Assembly Diagrams*. Join into diagonal rows; join rows to make quilt center.
2. Add top and bottom borders to quilt. Add side borders to quilt.

Quilting and Finishing

1. Divide backing fabric into 2 (2⅜-yard) lengths. Cut 1 piece in half lengthwise. Sew 1 narrow panel to each side of wide panel. Press seam allowances toward narrow panels.
2. Layer backing, batting, and quilt top; baste. Quilt as desired.

Quilt shown is quilted according to the fabric pattern in most pieces, with additional leaves, chevrons, and key patterns added.
3. Join 2¼"-wide black #12 strips into 1 continuous piece for straight-grain French-fold binding. Add binding to quilt.

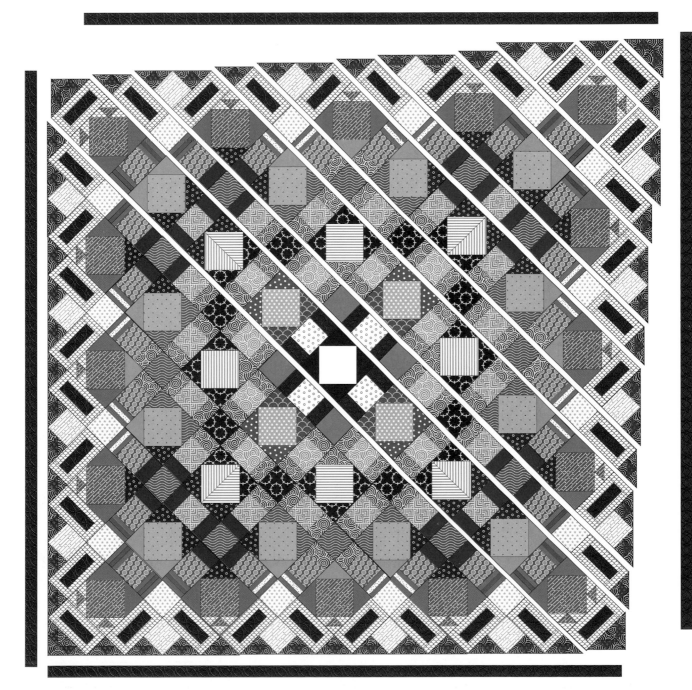

Quilt Top Assembly Diagram
(by color)

Traditions in Quilting

Barbara Barr
Littleton, Colorado

Making and designing quilts and talking to groups about quilts is an important part of Barbara Barr's life. "I give many volunteer hours to the Rocky Mountain Quilt Museum in Golden, Colorado," she says, "where I am a docent and have curated a couple of their gallery shows."

Barbara took her first stab at quilting when she was seven years old. She made several Four-Patch blocks, which her mother found and mailed to her

"A variety of fabrics is much more interesting than an organized selection."

about 20 years ago. "I designed a block around these Four-Patches and made my first quilt," Barbara recalls. "I was hooked for life!" Now Barbara makes both traditional and innovative art quilts, as well as creative clothing. Her fourth quilt, *Jones Pass,* was on the cover of *Quilter's Newsletter Magazine* and won 3rd Place in Amateur Quilts at the 1988 American Quilter's Society Show in Paducah, Kentucky. Another one of her quilts, consisting of eight original flower blocks, turned into a published book, *Cottonwood Pass.*

Barbara has been a member of the Colorado Quilting Council for 13 years and was inducted into their Hall of Fame in 1996. She also belongs to a small bee—The Fat Quarters—"And NO we're NOT!" she affirms.

In addition to quilting, Barbara enjoys the outdoors. "Living in Colorado gives me the chance to hike and climb," she says. "I also love to scuba dive, but in the warmer climes of the tropics!"

Spanish Tiles
2001

Barbara Barr loves scrap quilts. "A variety of fabrics is much more interesting than an organized selection," she says. "Using your stash brings back happy memories of your little girl's dresses, shirts made for your husband, or gifts and trades with friends. I love sorting the colors, and then arranging them in shades from lightest to darkest."

Spanish Tiles uses 181 different fabrics. Barbara assembled the main body of tesselated sawtooth squares before a trip to Spain.

"While in Spain, I photographed many of the tile designs on display in public places, and I used these photos as inspiration to create my border design," she says.

Spanish Tiles was juried into the 2002 American Quilter's Society Show in Paducah, Kentucky. It won 2nd Place in Large Pieced Quilts at the 2002 Piece in the Rockies Show in Colorado.

Spanish Tiles

Finished Size
Quilt: 77" x 91"
Blocks: 179 (4") squares with 1" sashing

Materials
99 (4½" x 10") pieces assorted dark prints for blocks (or 25 fat eighths*)

80 (4½" x 10") pieces assorted medium to light prints for blocks (or 20 fat eighths*)

3½ yards cream print for borders and binding

¼ yard (or 1 fat quarter**) teal print for appliqué

20 fat eighths* (or scraps) dark prints for appliqué

Black cord for couching

Variegated thread for quilting

5½ yards fabric for backing

Full-size batting

*Fat eighth = 9" x 22"

**Fat quarter = 18" x 22"

Editor's Note
This quilt requires careful color placement, as the color of one block is combined with adjacent blocks in the sashing strips. Ideally, you will need a design wall or other area to lay out the quilt pieces before assembling the quilt.

Cutting
Instructions are for rotary cutting and quick piecing. Cut pieces in order listed to make best use of yardage. Patterns are on pages 76–77.

From assorted dark prints, cut:
• 90 sets of 1 (4½") square, 1 (1½") corner square, and 8 (1⅞") squares.

• 9 sets of 1 (4½") square, 2 (1½") corner squares, and 8 (1⅞") squares.
Sets with 2 corner squares will be placed on the top row. You will need 99 dark sets total.

From assorted medium to light prints, cut:
• 72 light and medium sets of 1 (4½") square, 1 (1½") corner square, and 8 (1⅞") squares.
• 8 medium sets of 1 (4½") square, 2 (1½") corner squares, and 8 (1⅞") squares.
Sets with 2 corner squares will be placed on the top fill row. Light sets are to center, with medium sets filling to outside edges. You will need 80 light and medium sets total.

From cream print, cut:
• 8 (1⅞"-wide) strips. Cut strips into 152 (1⅞") squares for sashing units.
• 1 (1½"-wide) strip. Cut strips into 22 (1½") squares for sashing squares.
• 3 (8⅜"-wide) strips. Cut strips into 9 (8⅜") squares. Cut squares in quarters diagonally to make 36 side setting triangles.
• From remainder, cut 2 (5⅛") squares. Cut squares in half diagonally to make 4 corner setting triangles.
• 8 (6½"-wide) strips. Join in pairs to make 4 border strips.
• 9 (2¼"-wide) strips for binding.

From teal print, cut:
- 4 Ds, 4 Es, and 4 Es reversed for sides.

From assorted dark prints, cut:
- 4 different sets of 1 D, 1 A and 1 A reversed for corners.
- 4 different sets of 1 B and 1 C for corners.
- 4 different sets of 1 B reversed and 1 C reversed for corners.
- 2 different sets of 1 F, 1 G, and 1 H for sides.
- 2 different sets of 1 F reversed, 1 G reversed, and 1 H reversed for sides.
- 2 different sets of 1 I, 1 J, and 1 K for sides.
- 2 different sets of 1 I reversed, 1 J reversed, and 1 K reversed for sides.
- 2 different sets of 1 J and 1 K for top and bottom borders.
- 2 different sets of 1 J reversed and 1 K reversed for top and bottom borders.
- 2 different sets of 1 G and 1 H reversed for top and bottom borders.
- 2 different sets of 1 G reversed and 1 H for top and bottom borders.

Quilt Layout

Referring to photo and to *Quilt Top Assembly Diagram*, lay out dark sets on point in 11 rows of 9 squares each. Keep sets together. Fill in with light and medium sets, with light sets toward center. Place sets of 2 cream squares around sides of outer sets.

Sashing Strip Assembly

1. Starting with pieces for top left corner of quilt and referring to *Half-Triangle Unit Assembly*

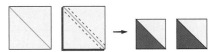

Half-Triangle Unit Assembly Diagrams

Diagrams, place 1 cream 1⅞" square atop 1 dark square, right sides facing. Draw a light line from corner to corner with a pencil. Stitch ¼" from drawn line on each side. Cut on drawn line and press open to make 2 half-square triangle units. Make 4 half-square triangle units. Join as shown in *Sashing Strip Assembly Diagram* to make sashing strip. Make 3 sashing strips with dark and cream

Sashing Strip Assembly Diagram

squares, and 1 sashing strip with dark and adjoining medium squares, orienting triangles as shown. Lay in position as shown in *Block Placement Diagram*. Place 1 dark square at top and bottom of center square. Place 1 cream square to left and 1 light square from lower right set to right.

2. For next top dark set to the right, make 2 sashing strips in cream and dark for top of square, 1 sashing strip with dark and adjoining bottom right medium squares, and 1 sashing strip with

Block Placement Diagram

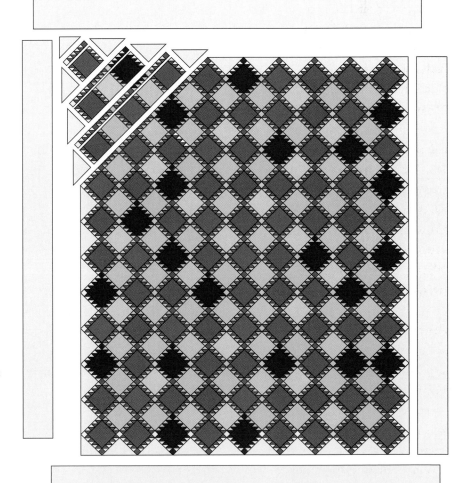

Quilt Top Assembly Diagram

Unit Placement Diagram

dark and adjoining bottom left medium squares. Lay in position as shown in *Unit Placement Diagram.*

3. Continue in same manner for all sets. Top row and top fill row each have 2 squares to match at top and bottom. All other units have matching square only at bottom.

Quilt Assembly

1. Blocks and sashing strips should be in proper position. Add setting triangles to edges of layout. Join into diagonal rows as shown in *Quilt Top Assembly Diagram.* Join rows to complete quilt center.

2. Measure length of quilt through center. Trim 2 border strips to this measurement and add to sides of quilt. Measure width of quilt, including side borders. Trim remaining border strips to this measurement and add to top and bottom.

3. Appliqué 1 A and 1 A reverse in each border corner. Add 1 D, 1 set of 1 B and 1 C, and 1 set of 1 B reversed and 1 C reversed.

4. Appliqué 1 E, 1 E reversed, and 1 D to center of each border. For each side, add 1 set of 1 F, 1 G, and 1 H, 1 set of 1 F reversed, 1 G reversed, and 1 H reversed, 1 set of 1 I, 1 J, and 1 K, and 1 set of 1 I reversed, 1 J reversed, and 1 K reversed.

5. For top, add 1 set of 1 G and 1 H reversed, 1 set of 1 G reversed and 1 H, 1 set of 1 J and 1 K, and 1 set of 1 J reversed and 1 K reversed. Repeat for bottom.

6. Couch stems with black cording and thread. Stem stitch or machine embroider details as shown in photo on page 74.

Quilting and Finishing

1. Divide backing fabric into 2 (2¾-yard) lengths. Cut 1 piece in half lengthwise. Sew 1 narrow panel to each side of wide panel. Press seam allowances toward narrow panels.

2. Layer backing, batting, and quilt top; baste. Quilt as desired. Quilt shown is quilted in variegated thread in blocks in a narrow quarter square pattern. In border, leaves are quilted in to match appliqué, then background is filled with narrow echo quilting.

3. Join 2¼"-wide cream strips into 1 continuous piece for straight-grain French-fold binding. Add binding to quilt.

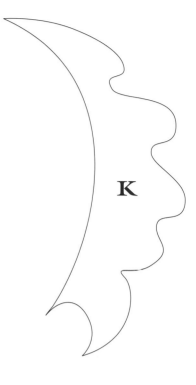

K

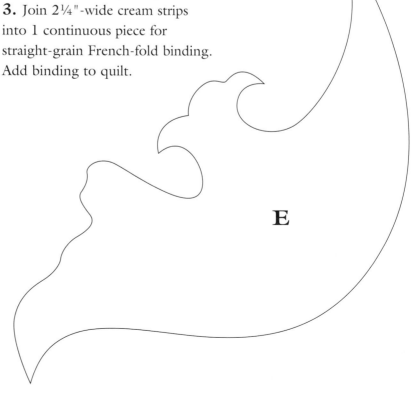

E

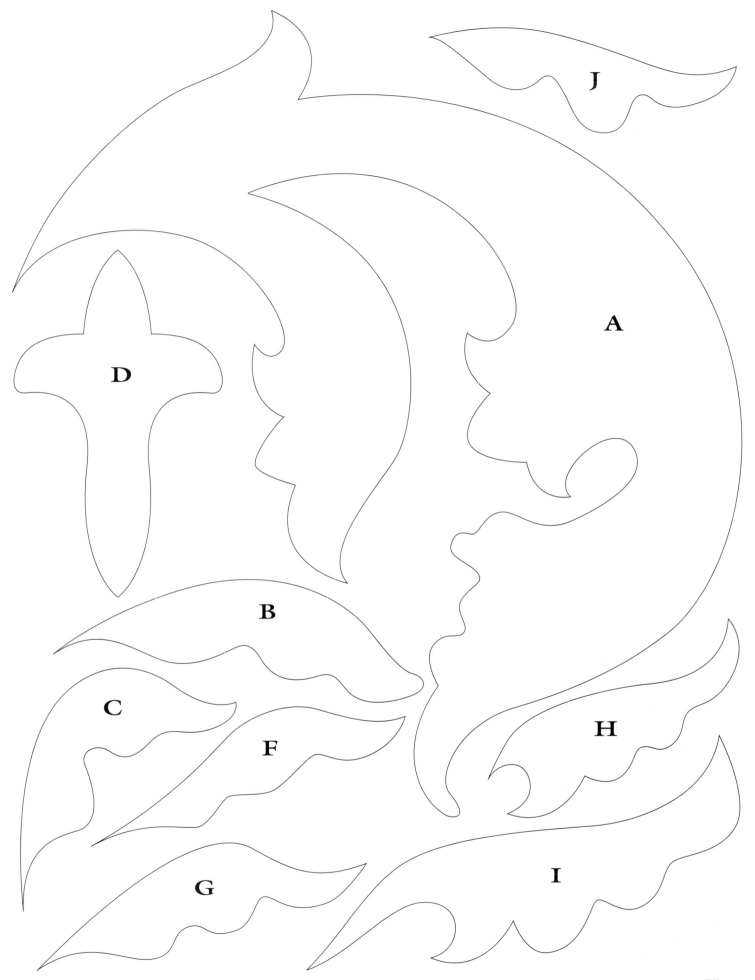

Elizabeth Spannring
La Center, Washington

Elizabeth Spannring is no stranger to the sewing machine. She has been quilting for more than 14 years. In the 10 years prior to that, she sewed clothing and crafts. Her vast experience has led her to a successful quilting career that includes teaching, lecturing, and judging in Washington, Oregon, Idaho, California, and Nevada.

"Quilting is my passion," Elizabeth says. "I spend 30 to 40 hours a week in quilt-related activities. I teach, design patterns, and make quilts for competition.

> *"Machine-quilting is my favorite part of the process. Anything I can do by machine makes me happy!"*

Machine-quilting is my favorite part of the process. Anything I can do by machine makes me happy! For me, this includes quilting, appliqué, and trapunto. Piecing is a challenge for me, although I do love the design process. Luckily, I like to machine-quilt so much, it forces me to get the top pieced!"

Elizabeth is active in several quilting guilds and organizations, including the Ladies of the Lake Guild in Longview, Washington; the Clark County Quilters of Vancouver, Washington; the International Quilt Association; the American Quilter's Society; and the Association of Pacific Northwest Quilters.

In 2002, Elizabeth completed a course on Judging Quilts and Wearable Arts sponsored by the Northern California Quilt Council. She also completed a continuing education program on Judging Innovative Quilts and Wearables. She recently judged the 2002 Northwest Quilting Expo in Portland, Oregon.

I'm in Love with Perry Winkle
2002

Elizabeth is especially fond of traditional quilts. "I am always looking for new ideas to showcase machine trapunto and machine quilting," she says.

The blocks used in *I'm in Love with Perry Winkle* are Elizabeth's variation of the Folk Fans block in Electric Quilt's block base by Barbara Brackman.

"I love the color periwinkle," Elizabeth says. "I found the fabric at a local quilt shop and knew immediately I would use it in my next quilt!"

Elizabeth's master machine work won several awards for *I'm in Love with Perry Winkle,* including a 3rd Place Machine-Quilting Merit Award at the 2002 International Quilt Festival in Houston, Texas, and a 1st Place ribbon in Traditional Pieced Quilts at the 2002 Great Pacific Northwest Quilt Show in Seattle, Washington.

I'm in Love with Perry Winkle

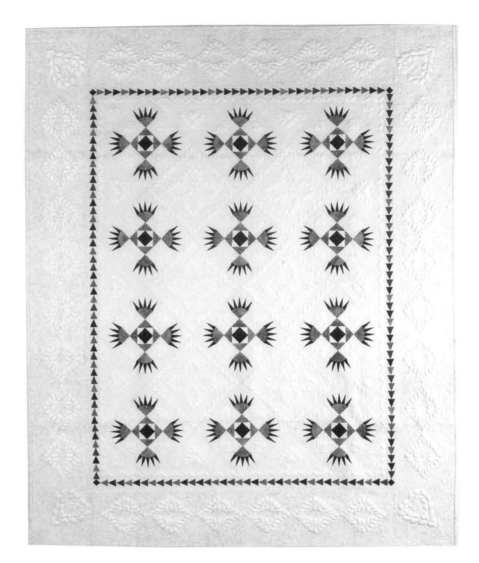

Finished Size
Quilt: 73¾" x 90¾"
Blocks: 12 (12") Blocks

Materials
¾ yard light blue
⅜ yard medium blue
¾ yard dark blue
8 yards cream-with-gold
¾ yard cream for binding
5½ yards fabric for backing
Full-size batting

Cutting
Instructions are for rotary cutting and quick piecing. Cut pieces in order listed to make best use of yardage. Border strips are exact length needed. You may want to cut them longer to allow for piecing variations. Patterns are on pages 82–83. Use more blue fabrics or scraps to increase variety in border strips.

From light blue, cut:
- 48 As for blocks.
- 2 (2⅞"-wide) strips. Cut strips into 24 (2⅞") squares. Cut squares in half diagonally to make 48 E triangles for blocks.
- 3 (2"-wide) strips. Cut strips into 56 (2") squares for border strips.

From medium blue, cut:
- 1 (2½"-wide) strip. Cut strip into 12 (2½") C squares for block centers.
- 3 (2"-wide) strips. Cut strips into 56 (2") squares for border strips.

From dark blue, cut:
- 15 (1¼"-wide) strips. Cut strips into 240 (1¼" x 2½") rectangles for arc points.
- 3 (2"-wide) strips. Cut strips into 60 (2") squares for border strips.

From cream-with-gold, cut:
- 2⅝ yards. Cut yardage into 2 (10½"-wide) lengthwise strips. Trim strips to make 2 (10½" x 91¼") outer side borders. From remainder, cut 6 (12½") setting squares. Also from remainder, cut 2 (9½") squares. Cut 9½" squares in half diagonally to make 4 corner setting triangles.
- 1⅝ yards. Cut yardage into

2 (10½"-wide) lengthwise strips. Trim strips to make 2 (10½" x 54¼") top and bottom outer borders. From remainder, cut 3 (18½") squares. Cut squares in quarters diagonally to make 12 side setting triangles. You will have 2 extra.
- 18 (2"-wide) strips. Cut strips into 288 (2" x 2½") rectangles for arc units.
- 48 Bs for blocks.
- 2 (2⅜"-wide) strips. Cut strips into 24 (2⅜") squares. Cut squares in half diagonally to make 48 D triangles for block centers.
- 6 (4½"-wide) strips. Cut strips

into 48 (4½") F squares for blocks.

- 17 (1¼"-wide) strips. Cut strips into 336 (1¼" x 2") rectangles for border strips.
- 1 (1¼"-wide) strip. Cut strip into 16 (1¼") squares for border corner units.

From cream, cut:

- 9 (2¼"-wide) strips for binding.

Block Assembly

1. Trace, scan, or photocopy 48 arc paper-piecing patterns. Paper-piece arc, beginning with cream for #1 and dark blue for #2. Use cream again for #3 and dark blue for #4. Continue in this manner until arc is complete. Trim excess seam allowance. Referring to *Corner Unit Assembly Diagram,* add 1 light blue A and 1 cream B to complete 1 corner arc unit. Make 4 corner arc units.

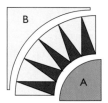

Corner Unit Assembly Diagram

2. Referring to *Center Unit Assembly Diagram,* join 1 D triangle to each side of 1 C square, working in opposite pairs. Join 1 E triangle to each side of C/D unit to complete 1 center unit.

Center Unit Assembly Diagram

3. Lay out corner and center units with 4 F squares as shown in *Block Assembly Diagram.* Join into rows; join rows to complete 1 block. Make 12 blocks.

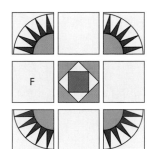

Block Assembly Diagram

Block Diagram

4. Trace, scan, or photocopy 28 border strip paper-piecing patterns. Paper-piece 1 border strip, using assorted blue squares for arrows and cream for background. Make 28 border strips.

5. Trace, scan, or photocopy 4 border corner paper-piecing patterns. Paper-piece 4 border corners, using dark blue for #1 centers and cream for background areas 2–5.

Quilt Assembly

1. Lay out blocks and setting pieces as shown in *Quilt Top Assembly Diagram.* Join into diag-

Quilt Top Assembly Diagram

onal rows; join rows to complete quilt center.

2. Join 8 (6-unit) border strips to make 1 side border. Repeat. Add to sides of quilt, noting direction of arrows.

3. Join 6 (6-unit) border strips. Add 1 border corner block to each end, as shown in *Border Unit Assembly Diagram*. Repeat. Add to top and bottom of quilt,

Border Unit Assembly Diagram

noting direction of arrows.

4. Add top and bottom cream borders to quilt. Add side borders.

Quilting and Finishing

1. Divide backing fabric into 2 (2¾-yard) lengths. Cut 1 piece in half lengthwise. Sew 1 narrow panel to each side of wide panel. Press seam allowances toward narrow panels.

2. Layer backing, batting, and quilt top; baste. Quilt as desired. Quilt shown is heavily quilted with extensive use of trapunto work.

3. Join 2¼"-wide cream strips into 1 continuous piece for straight-grain French-fold binding. Add binding to quilt.

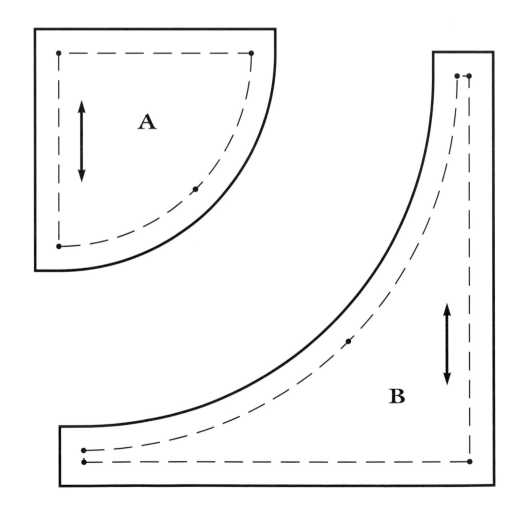

Paper Piecing

Place fabric #1 on wrong side of pattern, with wrong sides facing. Align fabric #2 with seam line so that it will flip over and cover area #2 after stitching. With right sides together, stitch along line between #1 and #2. Trim seam allowance, if needed, and flip #2 in place. Finger-press seam. Continue in numerical order. When paper pattern is complete, trim along seam allowance, remove paper, and press piece.

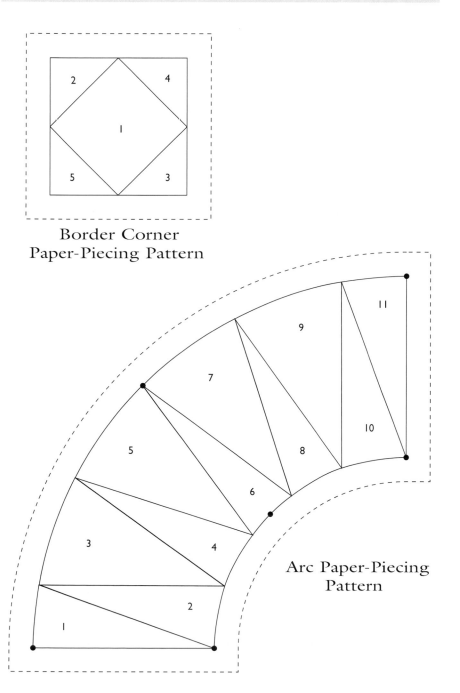

Border Corner
Paper-Piecing Pattern

Arc Paper-Piecing
Pattern

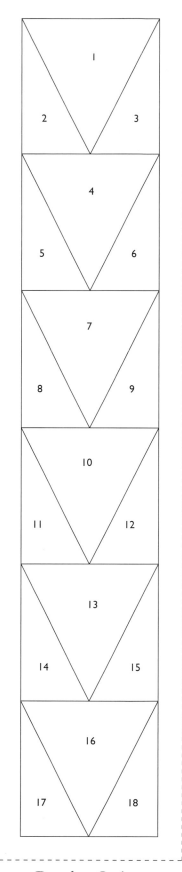

Border Strip
Paper-Piecing Pattern

Paulette Peters
Elkhorn, Nebraska

*P*aulette Peters began quilting in the 1970s, desiring the connection that quilting provides with generations of women's history and art. "My own family had no quilters, so this was a new experience," says Paulette. "I've found wonderful friendships and shared interests with my own generation as well as the young women who are discovering quilting now."

Paulette is a passionate quilter who has taught quiltmaking on the national level, designed numerous fundraising quilts, and written four quilting books. "I quilt almost every day and find it to be a great means of expression," says Paulette. "I piece, appliqué, and quilt either by hand

> *"I like to express an idea or record an experience in my quilts."*

or machine, using the most appropriate method for the piece. I would say that I'm a contemporary quilter—part traditional, part innovative. I like to express an idea or record an experience in my quilts."

In addition to her other activities, Paulette has served as past president for both the Nebraska State Quilt Guild and the Cottonwood Quilters of Nebraska. *Arachne* was the first quilt she submitted to Houston, and it took home a 3rd Place ribbon.

Arachne
2002

Arachne was juried into the 2002 International Quilt Festival in Houston, Texas, where it won 3rd Place in Mixed Techniques.

Two antique quilts in Paulette's collection inspired this quilt. "Both of the quilts are sometimes known as Spider Web," says Paulette. "They are in terrible condition, and I had always promised myself to make one of my own. As I worked on the geometric blocks, I felt they needed a softer border to balance the sharp angles and lines. Thinking of where webs might be found led me to design the tangled foliage for the edge."

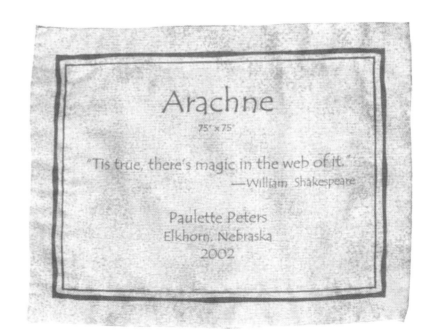

The title, *Arachne*, is the name of the mythological woman whose pride in her handwork led Athena to turn her into a spider.

"The name is a warning about pride," says Paulette, "or maybe the moral of the story is, 'Never annoy a goddess.'"

Arachne

Finished Size
Quilt: 74½" x 74½"
Blocks: 16 (14⅞") Spider Web Blocks

Materials
8 yards total assorted light cream and gray prints for blocks and borders
4 yards total assorted dark prints for blocks and appliqué
⅝ yard rust brocade for inner border appliqué
1½ yards blue batik for appliqué stems
2 yards total assorted dark large prints for appliqué
4½ yards fabric for backing
Full-size batting

Cutting
Cut pieces in order listed to make best use of yardage. Patterns are on pages 88–91.

From assorted light cream and gray prints, cut:
- 16 sets of:
  - 4 (5⅞") squares. Cut squares in half diagonally to make 8 D triangles.
  - 48 (1½" x 2½") A rectangles.
  - 5 (2⅜") squares. Cut squares in half diagonally to make 10 C triangles. You will have extras for most blocks.
- 9 (8"-wide) strips (or equivalent). Cut strips into random widths ranging from 3½" to 8" for borders.
- 9 (2¼"-wide) strips for binding. Use shorter lengths for more variety.

From assorted dark prints, cut:
- 16 sets of 8 Es.
- 1536 (1½") B squares.
- 23 (2⅜") squares. Cut in half diagonally to make 46 C triangles for blocks.

From rust brocade, cut:
- 8 (2"-wide) strips. Join in pairs to make 4 inner border strips for appliqué.

From blue batik, cut:
- 28 yards of ¾"-wide bias strips. Fold and press to make bias for border stems. You will need 32 (3") sections, 32 (4") sections, 80 (5") sections, 24 (9") sections, and 8 (14") sections.

From assorted dark large prints, cut:
- 4 Fs.
- 32 Gs and 32 Gs reversed.
- 68 Hs.
- 40 Is.
- 48 Js.

Block Assembly

1. Referring to *Diagonal Seams Diagram*, place 1 B atop 1 end of 1 A. Stitch diagonally from corner to corner. Trim excess fabric ¼" from stitching. Press open to reveal triangle. Repeat on opposite end of A to make 1 Goose Chase unit. Make 48 Goose Chase units with matching As and assorted Bs.

Diagonal Seams Diagram

2. Join 5 Goose Chase units as shown in *Side Unit Assembly Diagram* to make 1 side strip. Make 4 side strips.

Side Unit Assembly Diagram

3. Join 7 Goose Chase units to make 1 corner unit strip. Make 4 corner unit strips.

4. Referring to *Corner Unit Assembly Diagram*, add 1 D triangle to each side of 1 corner unit strip. Add 1 light C to inner corner. Add 1 dark C to outer corner to complete 1 corner unit. Make 4 corner units.

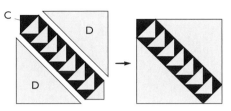

Corner Unit Assembly Diagram

5. Referring to *Center Star Unit Assembly Diagram*, join 2 Es and 1 light C as shown to make 1 point unit. Make 4 point units. Join point units to make center star unit.

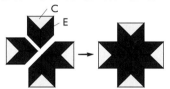

Center Star Unit Assembly Diagram

6. Lay out center star, side strips, and corner units as shown in *Block Assembly Diagram*. Join side strips

Block Assembly Diagram

to center star. Set in corner units to complete 1 Spider Web block (*Block Diagram*).

7. Make 16 Spider Web blocks. Make 2 blocks with 4 dark Cs in

Block Diagram

outer corners. These will be placed in upper left and lower right corners of quilt top. Make 4 blocks with 2 opposite dark Cs. These will be placed in the center of quilt top. Make 10 blocks with 3 dark and 1 light C corners. These will be rotated into position on edges of quilt top.

Quilt Assembly

1. Lay out blocks, placing and rotating as shown in *Quilt Top Assembly Diagram*. Join into rows; join rows to complete quilt center.

2. Join assorted light 8" pieces to make 1 (8" x 80") border strip. Make 4 border strips. Pin 1 rust strip in place on inner edge, as shown in *Appliqué Placement Diagram*.

3. Center 1 border strip on each side of quilt and join. Miter corners.

For Steps 4 and 5, refer carefully to Appliqué Placement Diagrams.

4. Arrange vines for appliqué. Stitch inner edge of vine in place, sewing through rust border and securing it to light border. Trim excess rust border beyond vines,

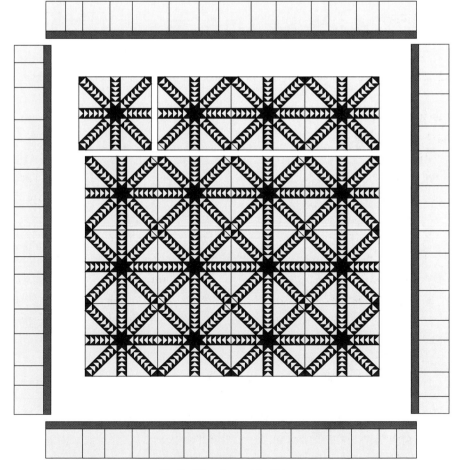

Quilt Top Assembly Diagram

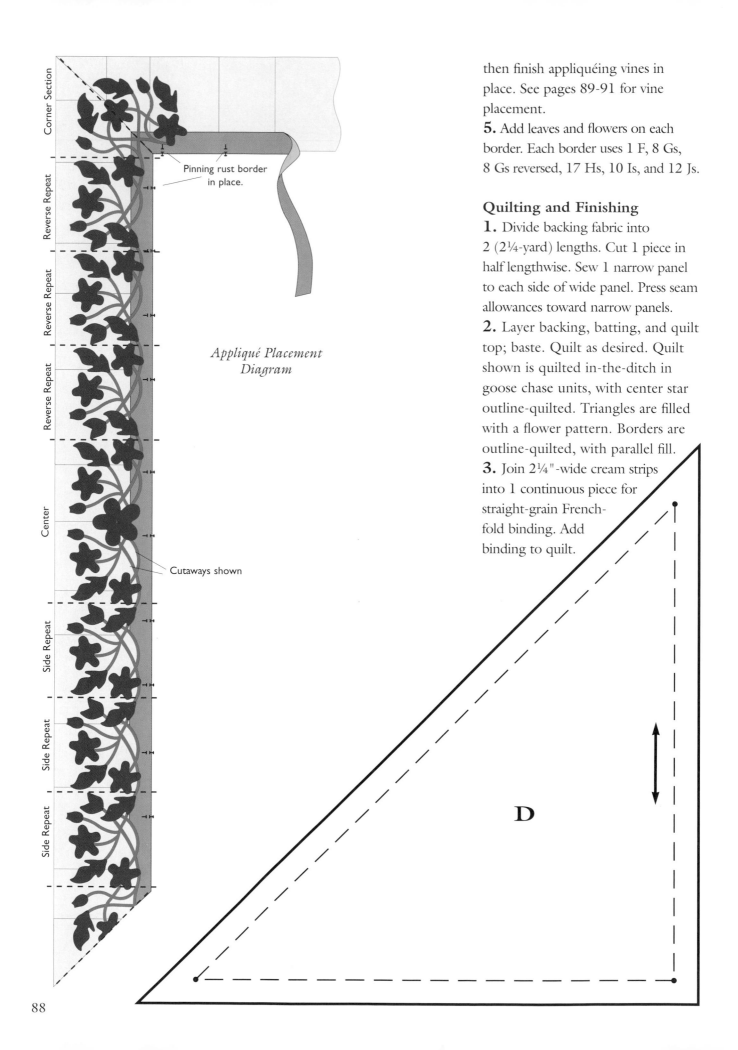

Corner Section

Reverse Repeat

Reverse Repeat

Reverse Repeat

Center

Side Repeat

Side Repeat

Side Repeat

Pinning rust border
in place.

*Appliqué Placement
Diagram*

Cutaways shown

then finish appliquéing vines in
place. See pages 89-91 for vine
placement.

5. Add leaves and flowers on each
border. Each border uses 1 F, 8 Gs,
8 Gs reversed, 17 Hs, 10 Is, and 12 Js.

Quilting and Finishing

1. Divide backing fabric into
2 (2¼-yard) lengths. Cut 1 piece in
half lengthwise. Sew 1 narrow panel
to each side of wide panel. Press seam
allowances toward narrow panels.

2. Layer backing, batting, and quilt
top; baste. Quilt as desired. Quilt
shown is quilted in-the-ditch in
goose chase units, with center star
outline-quilted. Triangles are filled
with a flower pattern. Borders are
outline-quilted, with parallel fill.

3. Join 2¼"-wide cream strips
into 1 continuous piece for
straight-grain French-
fold binding. Add
binding to quilt.

D

H

G

H

Side Border Appliqué Placement

J

J

I

G

H

Repeat along this line.

A

B

E

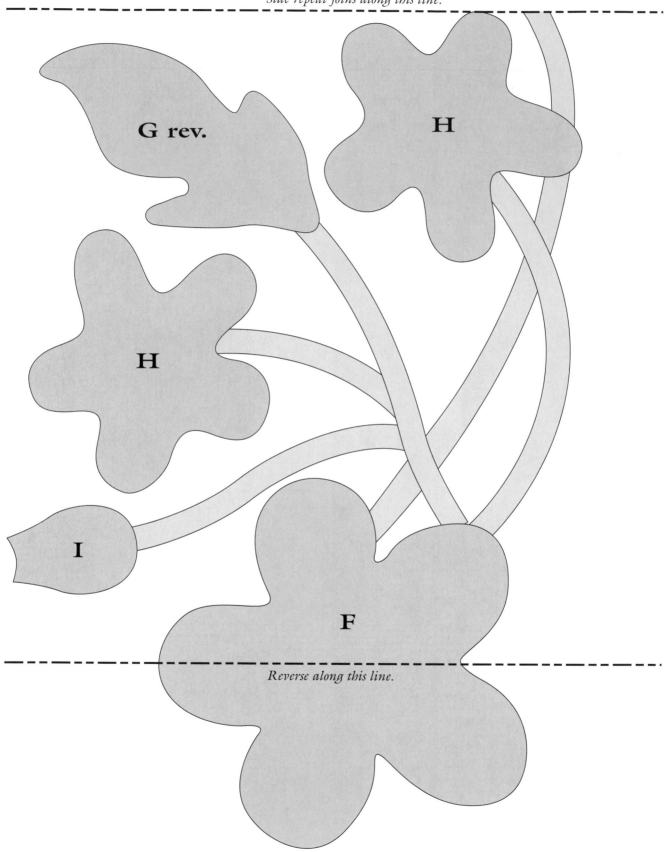

G rev.

H

H

I

F

Reverse along this line.

Center Appliqué Placement

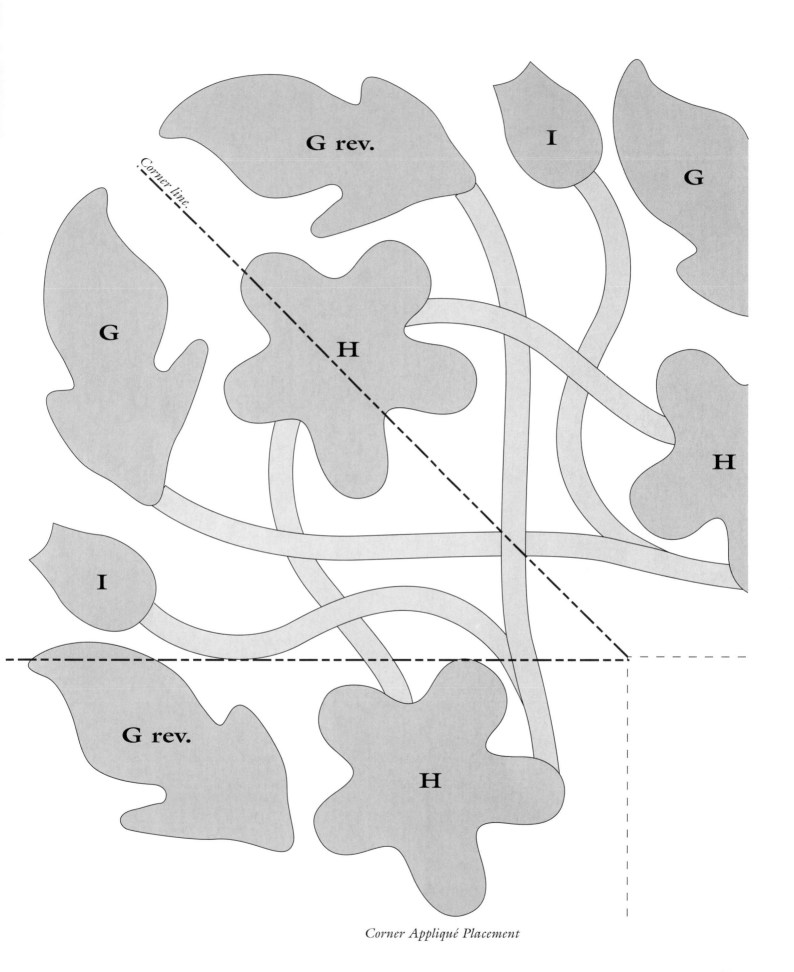

G rev.

I

G

Corner line.

G

H

H

I

G rev.

H

Corner Appliqué Placement

91

Carolyn Van de Graaf

Yakima, Washington

Carolyn Van de Graaf began quilting about 20 years ago when she found three of her grandmother's hand-pieced quilt tops, which were made in the late 1800s. "I had just gotten into the love of quilting, so it was both a goal and a challenge to finish them," says Carolyn. "First I had to learn how to hand quilt, which in those years, was the way most of us did it. I prefer hand-quilting to machine-quilting, but I do both."

Carolyn is a member of several quilting guilds, including the Horizon Quilters Unlimited of Yakima Valley in Grandview, the Yakima Valley Quilters Guild in Yakima, and the Quilting B at her church, which makes quilts for charities. "I enjoy the fellowship and friends I have met through quilting," she says.

Scrap quilts are Carolyn's favorites. She seldom makes any pattern twice, and enjoys using fabrics from her extensive reproduction print collection. "I love traditional patterns. The more difficult, the better," says Carolyn. "I love the challenge. I love the sense of accomplishment with each new, finished project. I feel it is almost a part of me."

> *"I love traditional patterns. The more difficult, the better. I love the challenge."*

Because she likes to keep her hands busy, Carolyn usually has several quilts going on at one time in different stages. She usually does handwork at night, so she can join her husband in the living room. She does exquisite work, and she has won ribbons in several major quilt shows. Although she chooses difficult patterns to stitch, Carolyn says that math is not her forté. "Quilting is therapy for me," she says.

Plaid Fantasy
2001

Carolyn saw an antique plaid quilt in a 1986 issue of *Ladies Circle Patchwork Quilts* that inspired the center of *Plaid Fantasy.* "I tried not to place two identical plaids or plaids in the same color next to each other," she says. "I have no idea how much yardage I used. I just cut out until I had enough pieces."

She later came across a Russion Sunflower block and decided to use it for a border. She used a different plaid fabric for each sunflower.

Carolyn hand-pieced and hand-quilted the entire quilt, except for the binding. It took her about two years to make it. "I enjoyed every part of it," she says.

Plaid Fantasy was exhibited at the 2001 Yakima Valley Quilters Guild Show. It won a blue ribbon at the 2001 Washington State Fair, and then was juried into the 2002 American Quilter's Society Show in Paducah, Kentucky. It was also published in *Quilter's Newsletter Magazine* in April 2003.

Plaid Fantasy

Finished Size
Quilt: 92" x 116"
Blocks: 176 (5") Tea Leaf Blocks,
28 (12½") Russian Sunflower
Blocks

Materials
20 yards muslin
10 yards total assorted plaids
7⅞ yards fabric for backing
King-size batting

Cutting
Instructions are for rotary cutting
and quick piecing. Cut pieces in
order listed to make best use of
yardage. Patterns are on pages
96-97.

From muslin, cut:
- 352 Bs.
- 54 Cs.
- 2 Ds.
- 69 (3"-wide) strips. Cut strips
  into 896 (3") squares for sunflower Fs and Gs.
- 13 (2⅞"-wide) strips. Cut strips
  into 174 (2⅞") squares for
  half-triangle blocks.
- 10 (13"-wide) strips. Cut strips
  into 28 (13") squares for sunflower blocks.
- 12 (2¼"-wide) strips for binding.

From plaids, cut:
- 759 As.
- 174 (2⅞") squares for half-
  triangle blocks.
- 28 sets of 16 (2" x 3½") E pieces
  and 1 H for sunflower blocks.

Block Assembly
1. Referring to *Tea Leaf Block
Assembly Diagram*, join 4 assorted
As to 1 B to make 1 Tea Leaf

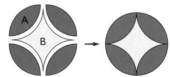

Tea Leaf Block Assembly Diagram

block. Make 176 Tea Leaf blocks.
2. Referring to *Half Block
Assembly Diagram*, join 2 As to 1
C to make 1 half block. Make 27
half blocks.

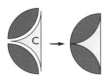

Half Block Assembly Diagram

3. Referring to *Half-Triangle
Assembly Diagram*, place 1 muslin
and 1 plaid squares right sides fac-

ing. Draw a line diagonally across
muslin. Stitch ¼" from drawn line
on both sides. Cut on drawn line
and open to make 2 half triangle
blocks. Make 348 half triangle
blocks for borders.

Half-Triangle Assembly Diagram

4. To make Russian Sunflower
blocks, choose 1 set of plaids.
Using paper piecing, position 1
plaid E, aligning with grain mark.
Place 1 F atop E so that when
stitched and opened, F will cover
the proper area. Stitch, open, and
finger-press. Repeat with 1 G to

94

complete 1 Sunflower section. Make 16 matching Sunflower sections (*Sunflower Section Diagram*).

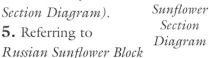

5. Referring to *Russian Sunflower Block Assembly Diagram*, join sections in

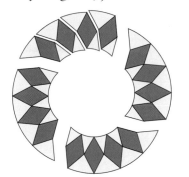

Sunflower Section Diagram

Russian Sunflower Block Assembly Diagram

groups of 4; join groups to make outer ring. Appliqué 1 H in center of ring. Appliqué sunflower in center of 1 (13") square to complete 1 Russian Sunflower block (*Block Diagram*).

6. Make 28 Russian Sunflower blocks.

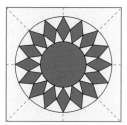

Russian Sunflower Block Diagram

Quilt Assembly

1. Lay out Tea Leaf blocks, half blocks, and fill pieces as shown in *Quilt Top Assembly Diagram*. Join into rows; join rows to complete quilt center.

2. Join 41 half triangle blocks to make left side border strip. Adjust seams as needed and join. Repeat for right side.

3. Join 31 half triangle blocks to make top border strip. Adjust seams as needed and join. Repeat for bottom strip.

4. Join 7 Russian Sunflower blocks to make 1 side strip. Adjust seams as needed and join to quilt. Repeat for opposite side, top and bottom.

5. Join 56 half triangle blocks to make left side outer border strip. Adjust seams as needed and join to quilt. Repeat for right side.

6. Join 46 half triangle blocks to make top outer border strip. Adjust seams as needed and join to quilt. Repeat for bottom strip.

Quilting and Finishing

1. Divide backing fabric into 3 (2⅞-yard) lengths. Join along sides to make backing. Seams will run horizontally.

2. Layer backing, batting, and quilt top; baste. Quilt as desired. Quilt shown is outline-quilted in B pieces, with borders and sunflowers quilted in-the-ditch. Sunflower centers and border are filled with diagonal grid quilting.

3. Join 2¼"-wide muslin strips into 1 continuous piece for straight-grain French-fold binding. Add binding to quilt.

Quilt Top Assembly Diagram

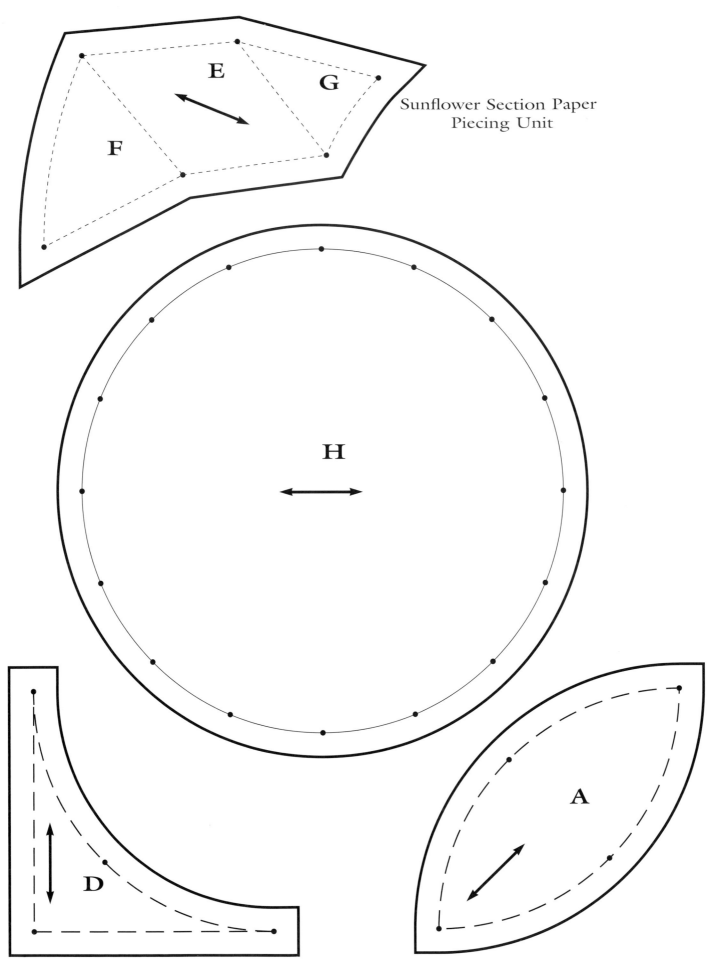

Sunflower Section Paper
Piecing Unit

E

G

F

H

D

A

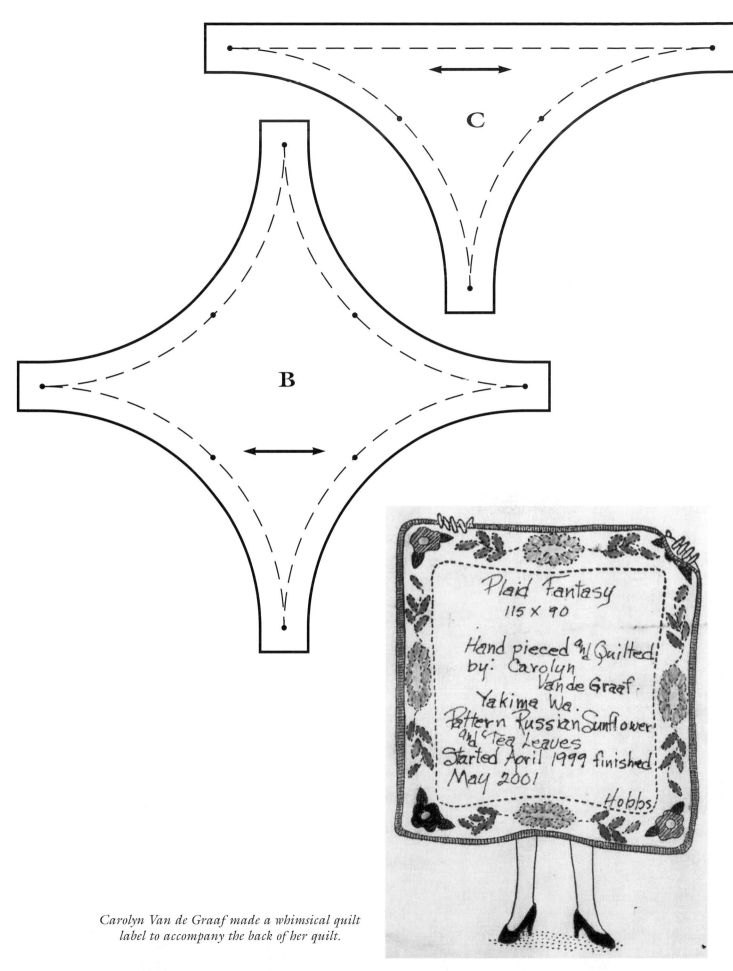

C

B

Plaid Fantasy
115 X 90

Hand pieced and Quilted
by: Carolyn
Van de Graaf.
Yakima Wa.
Pattern Russian Sunflower
and Tea Leaves
Started April 1999 finished
May 2001
Hobbs

Carolyn Van de Graaf made a whimsical quilt
label to accompany the back of her quilt.

Jill Schumacher
Weed, California

*J*ill Schumacher began sewing as a young girl. "My mother was a professional seamstress, and I have a special aunt, Margaret Cooke, who taught me how to make my first Nine-Patch quilt when I was 12," Jill says. "I have had the love of quilting in my heart ever since."

Jill moved to northern California in 1994 and wanted to start quilting again. She entered her first project in the county fair and won her first ribbon in 1996. This

"I find that quilting is a great way to unwind after a long day at work."

sparked her desire to learn machine quilting. After taking a local class, Jill found Diane Gaudynski's Web site on the Internet and began corresponding with her. "In 2000, I flew to Wisconsin and took her advanced machine academy, where I learned the trapunto technique," says Jill. "Since then, I have gone on to compete in Paducah at the American Quilter's Society Show, where I have won 2nd place awards for two consecutive years." Jill also won the Best Machine Quilting Award at the National Quilter's Association in 2001 and 2002.

In 1998, Jill started her own quilting business. She quilts about 45 quilts a year for customers and makes one competition quilt each year. She also works full-time at a community college, where she is the purchasing coordinator for computer and telecommunications equipment. "I find that quilting is a great way to unwind after a long day at work," says Jill. "It has brought great joy to me and my children, Steve, Dana, and Katherine, who have been my greatest fans. They have encouraged me to compete in the quilting world."

In My Garden: A Hummingbird Tale
2001

"Each spring, I have the pleasure of being visited by hummingbirds," says Jill. "I have several feeders hanging on my deck and have been able to count at least 150 birds during the peak season. I designed my quilt to express my love for both hummingbirds and the flowers that attract them to my garden—the lilac and wisteria.

I selected the green and purple fabrics to represent those flowers."

Jill machine-pieced and machine-quilted her work. She chose RJR sateen for the background because of its natural sheen. "It gives the quilt a look of morning light shimmering on the dew," she says.

Jill added trapunto to the machine designs and hummingbirds to give the quilt added dimension. She started the quilt on July 4, 2001, and finished it New Year's Eve, 2001. Jill estimates that she spent 850 hours on the quilt. But all her hard work paid off—the quilt won many awards in 2002. See page 102 for a complete list of honors.

In My Garden: A Hummingbird Tale

Finished Size

Quilt: 90" x 90"
Blocks: 8 (14³⁄₁₆") Feathered Star
Blocks

Materials

8 yards white sateen
1 fat quarter each light green,
    medium green, dark green,
    light purple, medium purple,
    and dark purple for star blocks
½ yard total assorted medium and
    dark green prints for inner
    border
¾ yard total assorted medium and
    dark purple prints for outer
    border
¾ yard purple for binding
8¼ yards fabric for backing
Queen-size batting

Cutting

Instructions are for rotary cutting and quick piecing. Cut pieces in order listed to make best use of yardage. Patterns are on page 103.

From white sateen, cut:

• 1⅝ yards. Cut yardage into
    2 (16½"-wide) lengthwise
    strips. Cut strips into
    2 (16½" x 54½") top and
    bottom borders.
• 2½ yards. Cut yardage into
    2 (16½"-wide) lengthwise
    strips. Cut strips into
    2 (16½" x 86½") side borders.
• 1 (14¹¹⁄₁₆"-wide) strip. Cut strip
    into 1 (14¹¹⁄₁₆") center square.
• From remainder, cut 24
    (2⅜" x 14¹¹⁄₁₆") sashing strips.
• 1 (2⅜"-wide) strip. Cut strip

into 16 (2⅜") sashing squares.
• 11 (2⅞"-wide) strips. Cut strips
    into 140 (2⅞") squares for
    triangle borders.
• 128 (1¹³⁄₁₆") squares (use template
    for star triangle quick piecing).
• 128 A triangles.
• 64 C triangles.
• 2 (7¼"-wide) strips. Cut strips
    into 8 (7¼") squares. Cut
    squares in quarters diagonally to
    make 32 E triangles.
• 32 F pieces.

From light green, cut:

• 32 B diamonds.
• 16 H triangles.
• 16 (2") J squares.

From medium green, cut:

• 32 Gs.

From dark green, cut:

• 64 (1¹³⁄₁₆") squares (use template
    for star triangle quick piecing).
• 32 D squares.
• 4 (4½") I squares.

*From assorted medium and dark
green prints, cut:*

• 52 (2⅞") squares for triangle
    border units. Use more fabrics
    for greater variety in border.

From light purple, cut:

• 32 B diamonds.
• 16 H triangles.
• 16 (2") J squares.

From medium purple, cut:

• 32 Gs.
• 4 (4½") I squares.

From dark purple, cut:

• 32 D squares.
• 64 (1¹³⁄₁₆") squares (template
    for star triangle quick piecing).

*From assorted medium and dark
purple prints, cut:*

• 88 (2⅞") squares for triangle
    border units. Use more fabrics
    for greater variety in border.

From purple, cut:

• 10 (2¼"-wide) strips for binding.

Block Assembly

1. Referring to *Half-Triangle Unit Assembly Diagram*, place 1 white square atop 1 dark green square, right sides facing, for star triangle quick piecing. Draw a line diagonally across white square back. Stitch ¼" on each side of line. Cut apart on drawn line and press open to make 2 half-square triangle units for star block. Make 32 half square triangle units.

Half-Triangle Unit Assembly Diagram

2. Join 2 half square triangle units and 1 white A triangle as shown in *A Unit Assembly Diagram* to make

A Unit Assembly Diagram

1 A unit strip. Repeat in opposite direction to make 1 A unit strip pair. Make 8 A unit strip pairs.

3. Referring to *A/B/C Unit Assembly Diagram*, join 1 B and 1 C as shown to end of 1 A unit strip. Repeat for opposite end of other strip as shown.

A/B/C Unit Assembly Diagram

4. Referring to *Side Unit Assembly Diagram*, join 1 unit strip to side of 1 E as shown. Add 1 D to end of remaining unit strip. Add to E as shown to make 1 side unit. Make 4 side units.

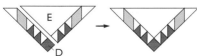

Side Unit Assembly Diagram

5. Referring to *Corner Unit Assembly Diagram*, add 1 A unit strip to bottom of 1 F as shown.

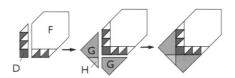

Corner Unit Assembly Diagram

Add 1 D to remaining unit strip and add to F. Add 1 G to bottom of unit. Join 1 G and 1 H as shown and add to complete 1 corner unit. Make 4 corner units.

6. Using diagonal seams and referring to *Center Unit Assembly Diagram*, place 1 J square on 1 corner of 1 I square. Stitch diagonally from corner to corner across diagonal of J. Trim excess fabric ¼" from stitching. Press open to reveal triangle. Repeat on all corners to make 1 center unit.

Center Unit Assembly Diagram

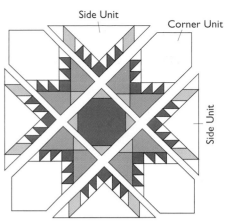

Block Assembly Diagram

7. Referring to *Block Assembly Diagram*, lay out center unit, side units, and corner units. Join into diagonal rows; join rows to complete 1 green Feathered Star block (*Block Diagram*).

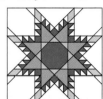

Block Diagram

8. Make 4 green and 4 purple Feathered Star blocks.

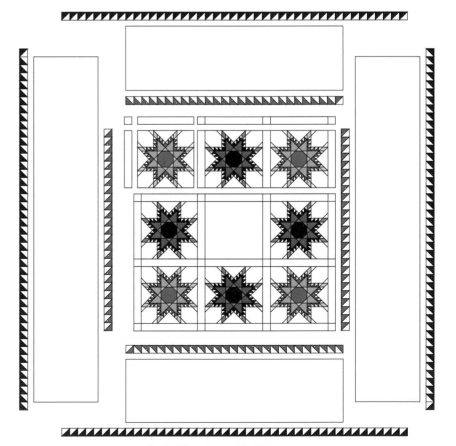

Quilt Top Assembly Diagram

101

Quilt Assembly

1. Lay out blocks, center square, sashing strips, and sashing squares as shown in *Quilt Top Assembly Diagram*. Join into rows; join rows to complete quilt center.

2. Referring to *Border Unit Assembly Diagram*, place 1 white square atop 1 dark green square, right sides facing, for border units. Draw a line diagonally across white square back. Stitch ¼" on each side of line. Cut apart on drawn line and press open to make 2 border units. Make 104 green border units and 176 purple border units.

Border Unit Assembly Diagram

3. Join 25 green border units as shown in *Quilt Top Assembly Diagram* for side border. Adjust seams as needed and join to quilt. Repeat for opposite border.

4. Join 27 green border units as shown for top border, noting orientation of last unit. Adjust seams as needed and join to quilt. Repeat for bottom border.

5. Add top and bottom white borders to quilt. Add side white borders to quilt.

6. Join 43 purple border units as shown for top border. Adjust seams as needed and join to quilt. Repeat for bottom border.

7. Join 45 purple border units as shown for side border, noting orientation of last unit. Adjust seams as needed and join to quilt. Repeat for opposite border.

Quilting and Finishing

1. Divide backing fabric into 3 (2¾-yard) lengths. Cut 1 piece in half lengthwise. Sew 1 narrow panel between wide panels. Press seam allowances toward narrow panel. Remaining panel is extra and may be used to make a hanging sleeve. Seams will run horizontally.

2. Layer backing, batting, and quilt top; baste. Quilt as desired. All quilt designs and hummingbirds in the quilt shown were quilted using trapunto. Blocks are quilted in-the-ditch, with cathedral window quilting in star tips, leaves in G pieces, and a hummingbird in each block center. More hummingbirds, feathered hearts, and swags are quilted into center area. Borders feature feathered ropes with hummingbirds. Background is heavily stipple quilted.

3. Join 2¼"-wide purple strips into 1 continuous piece for straight-grain French-fold binding. Add binding to quilt.

Honors & Awards

2002 American Quilter's Society Show in Paducah, Kentucky—2nd Place for Traditional Pieced, Professional

2002 National Quilt Association Show in North Carolina—Best Machine Quilting Award and 2nd Place for Traditional Pieced Bed Quilts

2002 Quilting the Quilt Show in Duluth, Minnesota—1st Place and Faculty Choice Award

2002 Mancuso World Textile Competition— Honorable Mention and Viewer's Choice

2002 Road to California Show in Ontario, Canada— 1st Place Traditional Pieced Bed Quilts

Close-up of Quilting

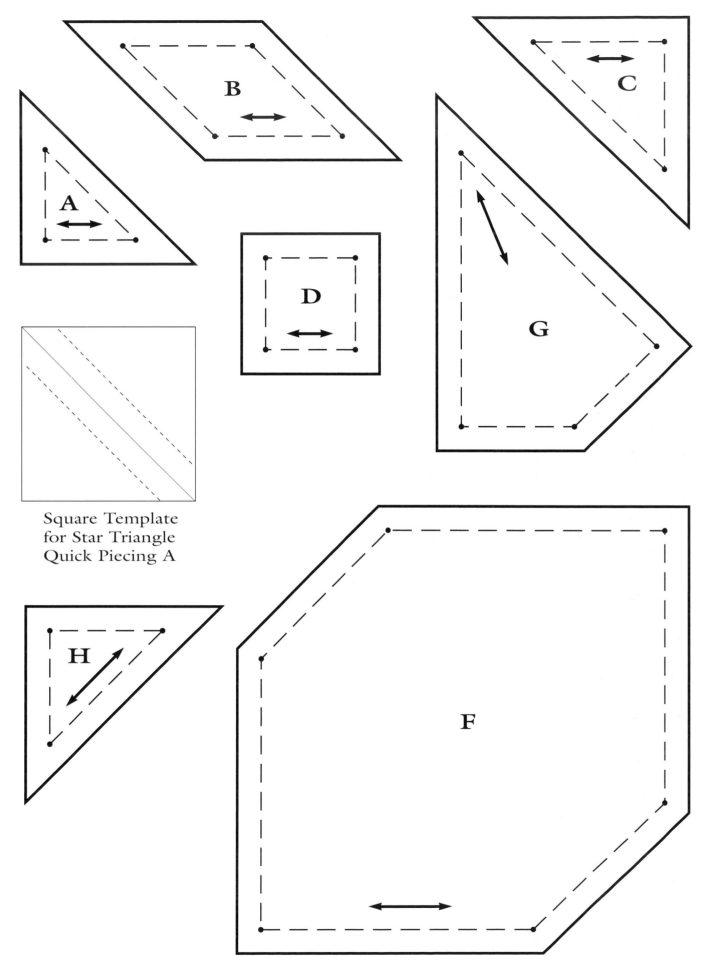

Square Template
for Star Triangle
Quick Piecing A

Bee
Quilters

Mediterranean Beauty

Serendipity

Beauty from Brokenness

I Like Red

Spring Has Sprung

Claudia Clark Myers
Duluth, Minnesota

Claudia Clark Myers began quilting in 1991, after her friend Jan dragged her to a quilt show. "She was sure I would love it," Claudia recalls, "and she was right!"

A retired costume designer of 25 years in opera, ballet, and the theater, Claudia enjoys the opportunity that quilting affords her to see her designs come to life—and to continue buying too much fabric! "I quilt almost every day—especially when I am in the clutches of creativity, or if there is a show deadline approaching." says Claudia. "I enjoy entering shows for the validation of my work, for the competition, and for the deadlines that I am used to working with. Without deadlines, I'd probably never get a quilt finished!"

Marilyn Badger
Brookings, Oregon

Photo courtesy of Dutch Drehmann

Marilyn Badger has been quilting for more than 25 years and producing award-winning quilts and garments on a longarm quilting machine since 1991.

She and her professional quilting techniques have been featured on multiple public television shows. She has taught longarm techniques for nine years in her private studio and various parts of the United States, Canada, and Australia. She has served as consultant for American Professional Quilting Systems and participated on their behalf at most major quilt shows over the years.

For information on her longarm quilting workshops, contact her at Oregon Coast Quilting, P.O. Box 1085, Brookings, OR 97415.

Mediterranean Beauty
2001

Claudia designed the "off-kilter New York Beauty" block for her paper-piecing pattern company, 2 Much Fun. Friend Barb Engelking designed the setting. Soon afterwards, Helen Smith Prekker asked Claudia to make a raffle quilt to benefit the Duluth YWCA. Joan Skalbeck, owner of Primrose Gradations, donated the hand-dyed fabric. Lavonne Horner created the over-dyed stripe fabric used in the border. Claudia decided this would be a great opportunity to do a trial run of the pattern before she published it, so she pieced the quilt top. Marilyn Badger did the exquisite machine quilting and suggested the name *Aegean Beauty*. Claudia countered with *Mediterranean Beauty*, and it seemed to fit. They raffled the quilt in July 2002 and made over $6,000.00 for the YWCA's programs for women. The quilt is now owned by Georgia Manthei of Petoskey, Michigan.

Mediterranean Beauty

Finished Size
Quilt: 104" x 104"
Blocks: 52 (9¾") Inner Blocks,
48 (8") Border Blocks

Materials
20 (¾-yard) pieces assorted hand-dyed solids in blue, purple, and green for backgrounds
20 (½-yard) pieces assorted hand dyed solids in green, gold, orange, and red for rays and backgrounds
1½ yards black-and-gold stripe for centers and outer blocks
2 yards blue-and-orange print for blocks
4 yards sky blue for background
1 yard solid teal for binding
9 yards fabric for backing
King-size batting

Cutting
Instructions are for rotary cutting and quick piecing. Cut pieces in order listed to make best use of yardage. Refer to photo for color combinations. Patterns are on pages 110–111.
From assorted hand-dyed solids in blue, purple, and green, cut:
• 41 Cs for block backgrounds.
• 52 sets of 8 (2½" x 6") rectangles for paper pieced ray background (odd numbers).
• 250 (13"-long) random-width (¾"–2" widths) strips for border blocks.
From assorted hand-dyed solids in green, gold, orange, and red, cut:
• 52 sets of 7 (2½" x 6") rectangles for paper pieced rays (even numbers).

• 250 (13"-long) random-width (¾"–2" widths) strips for border blocks.
From black-and-gold stripe, cut:
• 52 Bs for block centers. Stripes should align with grain arrow.
• 17 random width (¾"–2") strips. Cut strips into 50 (13"-long) random-width strips for border blocks.
From blue-and-orange print, cut:
• 52 As for blocks.
• 17 random-width (¾"–2") strips. Cut strips into 50 (13"-long) random-width strips for border blocks.
From sky blue, cut:
• 11 Cs for block backgrounds.
• 2 (33⅞") squares. Cut squares in half diagonally to make 4 corner triangles for background.
• 3 (10¼"-wide) strips. Cut strips into 4 (10¼" x 14") X rectangles and 4 (10¼") Y squares for background blocks.

From solid teal, cut:
• 12 (2¼"-wide) strips for binding.

Mediterranean Block Assembly
Refer to photo for color combinations.
1. Choose 1 set each of ray and ray background pieces. To paper-piece ray arc, place 1 ray background piece right side up on wrong side of pattern. Place 1 ray piece, right sides facing, atop first piece, aligning ¼" past line between #1 and #2 areas. Turn to right side of pattern and stitch along line. Flip open ray piece and finger-press. Fabric should cover area #2. Trim seam allowance to ¼" if needed. Repeat in numerical order, alternating ray pieces and background pieces, to complete 1 ray arc.
2. Add 1 A to arc as shown in *Block Assembly Diagram.* Add 1 B

to A. Add 1 C to outer edge of arc to complete 1 Mediterranean Beauty block *(Block Diagram)*. Remove paper and press block.

3. Make 52 Mediterranean Beauty blocks, using photo as a guide for color placement.

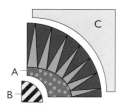 

Block Assembly Diagram   *Block Diagram*

Border Block Assembly

1. Referring to *Strip Piecing and Cutting Diagrams,* join strips at ran-

Strip Piecing and Cutting Diagrams

dom to make 1 (13") square. Trim square to 12⅝". Cut square in quarters diagonally to make 4 quarter-square triangles. Repeat to make 24 squares cut into 96 triangles.

2. Lay out 2 triangles that are pieced in opposite directions as shown in *Border Block Assembly Diagram.* Join to make 1 border block. Trim to 8½" square, if needed.

Border Block Assembly Diagram

3. Make 48 border blocks.

4. Referring to *Quilt Top Assembly Diagram,* join 11 border blocks to make left side border. Repeat for right side border.

5. Join 13 border blocks to make top border. Repeat for bottom border.

Quilt Assembly

Refer to *Quilt Top Assembly Diagram* throughout.

1. Lay out blocks in diagonal rows as shown. Center is made up of dark blocks, surrounded by lighter blocks. Outer blocks are darker. When satisfied with block placement, join blocks into diagonal rows. Add blue background blocks X and Y as shown. Join rows.

2. Add triangles to each corner, centering as shown, to complete quilt center. Trim quilt evenly to 88½" x 88½".

3. Add side borders to quilt, referring carefully to *Quilt Top Assembly Diagram* for placement. Add top and bottom borders.

Quilting and Finishing

1. Divide backing fabric into 3 (3-yard) lengths. Join along sides to make backing. Seams will run horizontally.

2. Layer backing, batting, and quilt top; baste. Quilt as desired. Quilt shown is quilted in concentric waves in centers, with rays quilted into points. Areas between points are heavily stippled. Background areas are quilted in petals and swirls, and the outer border is quilted in interlocking geometrics.

3. Join 2¼"-wide teal strips into 1 continuous piece for straight-grain French-fold binding. Add binding to quilt.

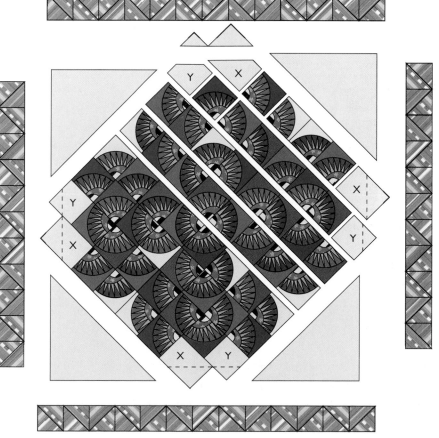

Quilt Top Assembly Diagram

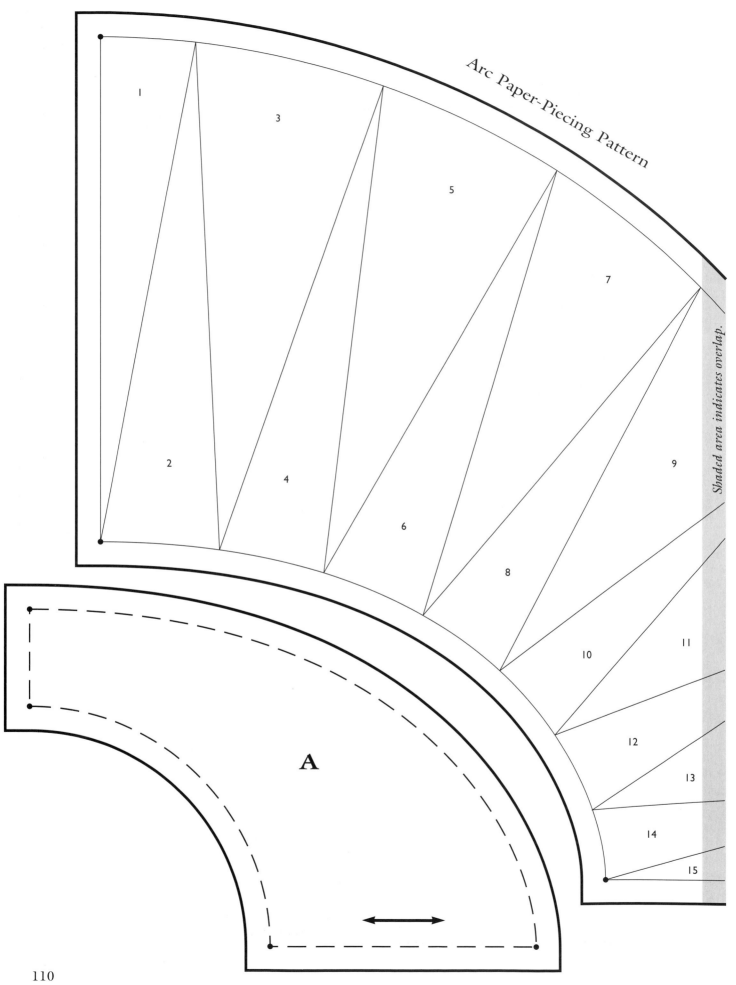

Arc Paper-Piecing Pattern

Shaded area indicates overlap.

1

3

5

7

9

2

4

6

8

11

10

12

13

14

15

A

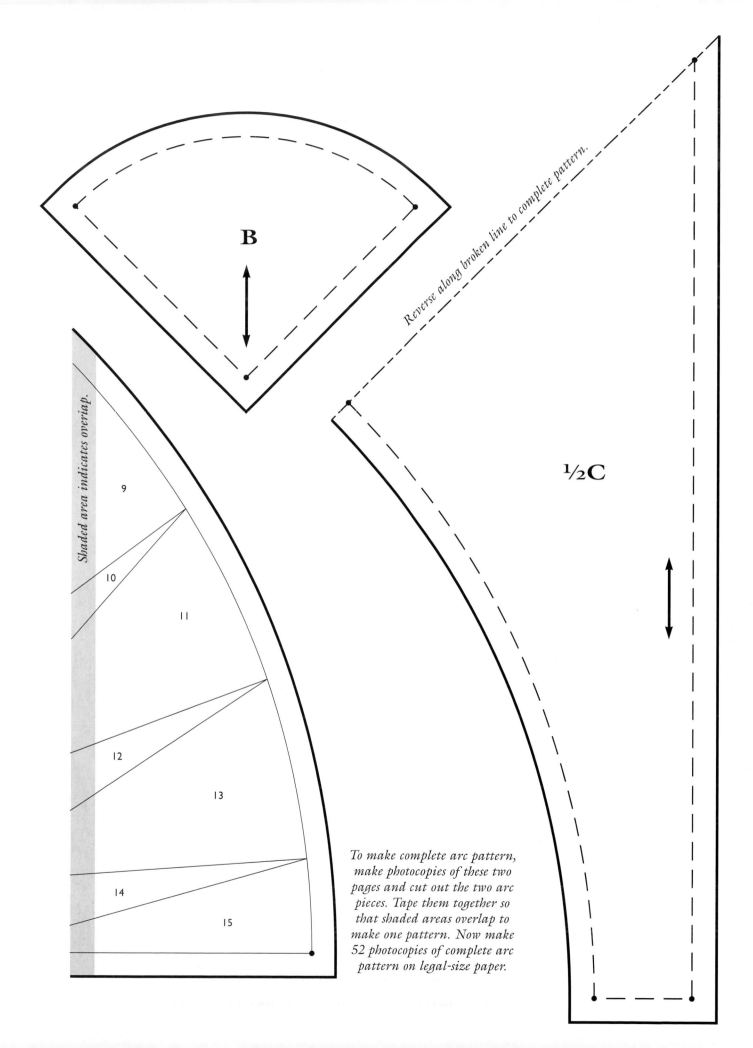

B

Reverse along broken line to complete pattern.

Shaded area indicates overlap.

½**C**

9

10

11

12

13

14

15

To make complete arc pattern, make photocopies of these two pages and cut out the two arc pieces. Tape them together so that shaded areas overlap to make one pattern. Now make 52 photocopies of complete arc pattern on legal-size paper.

Linda M. Roy
Pittsfield, Massachusetts

*L*inda Roy began quilting in 1989, while living in Conway, Arkansas. She met a new neighbor, Irma Gail Hatcher, who introduced her to the art. "Quilting is a creative outlet and passion for me," says Linda. "The friendships made along the way are incredibly special. It began as a hobby, but quickly became much more."

Linda belongs to several quilting organizations, including the American Quilter's Society, the International Quilt Association, the National Quilting Association, and the Yankee Pride Guild in Pittsfield, Massachusetts.

The quilt top that evolved into *Serendipity* began while Linda was living in Wisconsin. She and 11 close friends quilted together once a week for four years. Her

> *"Quilting is a creative outlet and passion for me. The friendships made along the way are incredibly special."*

buddies pooled their collection of red scraps and presented the top to Linda as a farewell gift when her family transferred to Mississippi. "It took three years for me to decide what quilting would do justice to the beautiful workmanship in this quilt," Linda confesses. "It's hard to believe they made it in only two days!" Ultimately, Linda hand-quilted the piece herself, adding trapunto to give the quilt extra dimension.

Serendipity
2001

Linda's friends who made the quilt top include Linda Webster, Jan Zinno, Sue Heuer, Pat Nigl, Barb Demerath, Dona Geeding, Kim Tiegen, Margaret Harness, Ellen Graf, Cathy Miller, and Judy Seaborn. Linda Roy did the spectacular hand quilting.

Serendipity has won awards in several major quilt shows. It won 1st Place and Judge's Choice at the 2001 Vermont Quilt Festival. It won the Hand Workmanship Award at the 2001 Pennsylvania National Quilt Extravaganza. And more recently, it took home a 1st Place ribbon at the 2002 National Quilt Association show in Greensboro, North Carolina.

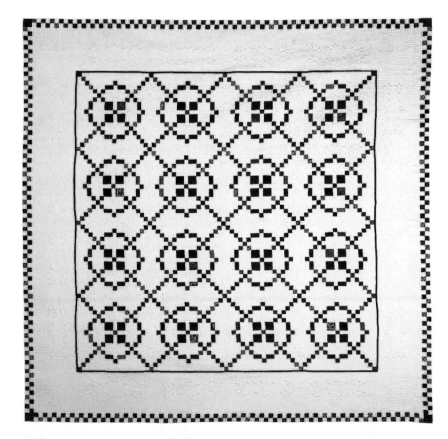

Serendipity

Finished Size

Quilt: 97" x 97"

Blocks: 16 (15") Burgoyne Surrounded Blocks

Materials

14 fat quarters (18" x 22") assorted red prints for blocks and pieced border (Use more for greater variety.)

¼ yard red print for inner appliquéd border

9½ yards white fabric for background and border

9 yards fabric for backing

King-size batting

Cutting

Instructions are for rotary cutting and quick piecing. Cut pieces in order listed to make best use of yardage.

From assorted red fat quarter prints, cut:

- 18 (2½" x 22") strips for center strip sets.
- 74 (1½" x 22") strips for center, block units, border, and sashing units strip sets.
- 4 (2½") assorted squares for outer border corners.

From 1 red print, cut:

- 8 (¾"-wide) strips for inner border appliqué. Join strips in pairs to make 4 border strips. Press long raw edges under ¼" to make ¼"-wide border strips for appliqué.

From white, cut:

- 2⅝ yards. Cut yardage into 4 (10½"-wide) lengthwise strips. Cut strips into 2 (10½" x 73½") side borders and

2 (10½" x 93½") top and bottom borders.

- 6 (2½"-wide) strips. Cut strips into 12 (2½" x 22") strips for center strip sets.
- 36 (1½"-wide) strips. Cut into 72 (1½" x 22") strips for center, block units, border, and sashing units strip sets.
- 17 (3½"-wide) strips. Cut strips into 64 (3½" x 5½") As and 128 (2½" x 3½") Bs for blocks.
- 12 (3½"-wide) strips. Cut strips into 24 (3½" x 15½") inner sashing strips.
- 8 (2½"-wide) strips. Cut strips into 16 (2½" x 15½") outer sashing strips.
- 11 (2¼"-wide) strips for binding.

Block Assembly

1. Referring to *Center Unit Red Strip Set Diagram*, join 2 (2½" x 22") assorted red strips to each side of 1 (1½" x 22") white strip to make 1 red center strip set. Make 9 red center strip sets. Cut strip sets into 32 (2½"-wide) segments and 64 (1½"-wide) segments.

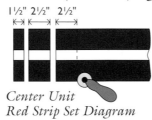

Center Unit Red Strip Set Diagram

2. Referring to *Center Unit White Strip Set Diagram*, join 2 (2½" x 22") white strips to each side of 1 (1½" x 22") red strip to make 1 white center strip set.

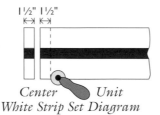

Center Unit White Strip Set Diagram

Make 6 white center strip sets with assorted red strips. Cut strip sets into 80 (1½"-wide) segments.

3. Referring to *Center Unit Assembly Diagram*, lay out 2 (2½"-wide) red segments with 1 (1½"-wide) white segment as shown. Join to make 1 center unit. Make 16 center units.

Center Unit Assembly Diagram

4. Referring to *Side Unit Assembly Diagram*, lay out 1 (1½"-wide) red segment with 1 (1½"-wide) white segment as shown. Join to make 1 side unit for blocks. Make 64 side units.

Side Unit Assembly Diagram

5. Referring to *Nine-Patch Red Strip Set Diagram*, join 2 (1½" x 22") assorted red strips to each side of 1 (1½" x 22") white strip to make 1 red Nine-Patch strip set. Make 12 red Nine-Patch strip sets. Cut strip sets into 158 (1½"-wide) segments.

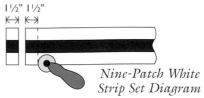

Nine-Patch Red Strip Set Diagram

6. Referring to *Nine-Patch White Strip Set Diagram*, join 2 (1½" x 22") white strips to each side of 1 (1½" x 22") red strip to make 1 white Nine-Patch strip set. Make 7 white Nine-Patch strip sets with assorted red strips. Cut strip sets into 85 (1½"-wide) segments.

7. Referring to *Nine-Patch Assembly*

Nine-Patch White Strip Set Diagram

Diagram, lay out 2 (1½"-wide) red segments with 1 (1½"-wide) white segment as shown. Join to make 1 Nine-Patch unit. Make 73 Nine-Patch units for blocks and sashing.

Nine-Patch Assembly Diagram

8. Referring to *Sashing Border Unit Assembly Diagram,* lay out 1 (1½"-wide) red segment with 1 (1½"-wide) white segment as shown. Join to make 1 side sashing unit. Make 12 side sashing units.

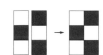

Sashing Border Unit Assembly Diagram

9. Referring to *Four-Patch Strip Set Assembly Diagram,* join 1 (1½" x 22") red strip to 1 (1½" x 22") white strip to make 1 Four-Patch strip set. Make 37 Four-Patch strip sets with assorted red strips. Cut strip sets into 508 (1½"-wide) segments.

Four-Patch Strip Set Assembly Diagram

10. Join 2 segments as shown in *Four-Patch Assembly Diagram* to make 1 Four-Patch unit. Make 68 Four-Patch units for blocks and sashing corners.

Four-Patch Assembly Diagram

11. Referring to *Border Assembly Diagram,* join 93 segments as shown, alternating direction, to make 1 outer border strip. Make 4 outer border strips.

Border Assembly Diagram

12. Referring to *Block Assembly Diagram,* lay out as shown: 1 center unit, 4 Nine-Patch units,

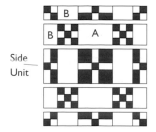

Block Assembly Diagram

4 As, 8 Bs, 4 side units, and 4 Four-Patch units. Join into rows; join rows to complete 1 Burgoyne Surrounded block *(Block Diagram).* Make 16 Burgoyne Surrounded blocks.

Quilt Assembly

Refer to *Quilt Top Assembly Diagram* throughout.

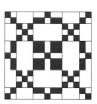

Block Diagram

1. Lay out blocks, sashing strips, and sashing square units as shown in *Quilt Top Assembly Diagram.* Join into rows; join rows to complete quilt center.

2. Join white side borders to quilt. Join top and bottom white borders to quilt.

3. Add 1 outer border strip to each side of quilt. Add 1 (2½") red square to ends of remaining strips. Add to top and bottom of quilt.

4. Appliqué red inner border to quilt, mitering corners. Border is ¼" wide.

Quilting and Finishing

1. Divide backing fabric into 3 (3-yard) lengths. Join along sides to make backing. Seams will run horizontally.

2. Layer backing, batting, and quilt top; baste. Quilt as desired. Quilt shown is quilted in-the-ditch around red pieces, with ¼" parallel quilting to fill blocks and background. Trapunto flowers surround the center units and in sashing, and flower patterns are repeated in border.

3. Join 2¼"-wide white strips into 1 continuous piece for straight-grain French-fold binding. Add binding to quilt.

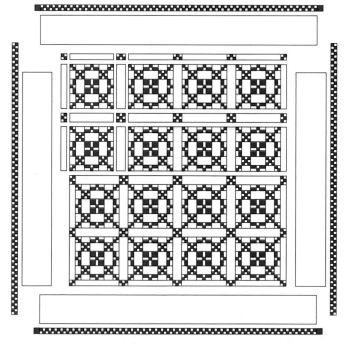

Quilt Top Assembly Diagram

Charlotte Roach
Stratford, Connecticut

The creation of this quilt spans a period of loss, grief, hope and eventually, renewal for Charlotte Roach. She began the quilt in 1998, shortly after her divorce. "Seeking solace in creativity, I started a fabric swap among the members of my Scrap Happy Charmers group," Charlotte recalls. "Every two weeks we would exchange 10 (6") blocks of a given color or fabric type. This gave me something to look forward to, and it provided the unique fabrics to create variety within my work."

Charlotte blended the colors together on her design wall. When she was ready to add the sashing, she used the fabrics from her former husband's discarded shirts.

"To me, this quilt was more than a bed covering, for it gave voice to my grief and to my hope for reconciliation.

The arrangement became rows of interlocking crosses. "I sometimes feel it looks like a cemetery of crosses, reminding me of the death of my marriage," says Charlotte. "Yet it also reveals to me a window of hope with the rainbow of colors that spring up in the background. To me, this quilt was more than a bed covering, for it gave voice to my grief and to my hope for reconciliation."

Charlotte chose words from Isaiah 61 for the border. Her former husband had succeeded in his career through his mastery of type fonts, so she selected an array of font styles for her lettering. She added the flowers and butterflies to symbolize life and freedom. The prairie points brought the number of quilt pieces to 2000, in celebration of the new millennium.

Beauty from Brokenness
2000

Charlotte Roach has been a member of the Connecticut Piecemakers Quilt Guild since 1994 and served as president from 2000–2002. She is also active in several satellite groups of this guild, including the Ladies of the Evening and the Scrap Happy Charmers.

Beauty from Brokenness has won awards in many local and national quilting shows, including:
• April 2000—Connecticut Piecemakers Quilt Show
• May 2000—Machine Quilters International Show in Illinois, President's Choice ribbon
• July 2000—Northeast Quilt Festival in Connecticut, 1st place ribbon
• September 2000—Juried into the Pennsylvania National Show

• May 2001—Northern Star Quilt Show in New York, 3rd place ribbon
• June 2001—New Jersey Quilt Convention, 2nd place ribbon
• August 2001—Juried into the World Quilt Show in Michigan and North Carolina
• April 2002—Juried into the Quilter's Heritage show in Lancaster, Pennsylvania

Beauty from Brokenness

Finished Size
Quilt: 88½" x 88½"
Blocks: 100 (6") Hourglass
Blocks

Materials
4 yards total assorted dark prints
3½ yards total assorted light prints
2½ yards total assorted light
    striped fabrics
2½ yards blue stripe for border
2 yards medieval print for letters
¼ yard total assorted scraps butter-
    fly and roses prints for appliqué
7⅞ yards backing
Queen-size batting
Metallic gold thread for embroidery

Cutting
Instructions are for rotary cutting and quick piecing. Cut pieces in order listed to make best use of yardage. For letters, choose a font from your computer or a design book and enlarge to an appropriate size.

From assorted dark prints, cut:
- 100 (3⅞") squares. Cut squares in half diagonally to make 200 A triangles.
- 400 (2") B squares.
- 121 (2") sashing squares.
- 165 (3") squares for prairie points.

From assorted light prints, cut:
- 100 (3⅞") squares. Cut squares in half diagonally to make 200 A triangles.
- 400 (2") B squares.
- 85 (3") squares for prairie points. You will need about 250 total.
- 16 border triangles.

From assorted light striped fabrics, cut:
- 220 (2" x 6½") sashing strips.

From blue stripe, cut:
- 4 (6½"-wide) lengthwise strips for border.

From medieval print, cut:
- Letters for border quote in an appropriate font. Uppercase letters should be approximately 4" high, with lowercase to scale and to fit border. The quote reads, "The LORD binds up the brokenhearted. HE adorns with joy those faint in despair. HE bestows a crown of beauty for ashes. HE looses the bonds of those in captivity."

From butterfly and rose prints, cut:
- 16 butterflies for border.
- 8 roses for border.

Block Assembly
1. Choose 2 light and 2 dark A triangles. Referring to *Triangle Unit Assembly Diagram*, join 1 of each to make 1 triangle unit. Make 2 triangle units.

Triangle Unit Assembly Diagram

2. Choose 4 light and 4 dark B squares. Referring to *Four-Patch Unit Assembly Diagram*, join 2 of each as shown to make 1 Four-Patch unit. Make 2 Four-Patch units.

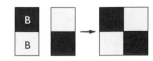

Four-Patch Unit Assembly Diagram

3. Lay out units as shown in *Block Assembly Diagram*. Join to make 1 Hourglass block *(Block Diagram)*. Make 100 Hourglass blocks.

Block Assembly Diagram   *Block Diagram*

Quilt Assembly

Refer to *Quilt Top Assembly Diagram* throughout.

1. Lay out blocks, sashing strips, and sashing squares as shown in *Quilt Top Assembly Diagram*. Join into rows; join rows to complete quilt center.

2. Center 1 blue border strip on each side of quilt and join. Miter corners.

3. Appliqué 4 light triangles on each side, centering on sashing squares, to complete lattice.

4. Using photo as a guide, appliqué letters for quotes on each border. Appliqué butterflies and roses to border as shown. Satin-stitch edges of each piece using metallic gold thread. Add antennae for butterflies in stem stitch.

Quilting and Finishing

1. Divide backing fabric into 3 (2⅝-yard) lengths. Join along sides to make backing. Seams will run horizontally.

2. Layer backing, batting, and quilt top; baste. Quilt as desired. Quilt shown is meander quilted in light areas, with seaweed patterns in dark triangles. Sashing strips have a frond pattern. Border has meander quilting to fill behind lettering.

3. Referring to *Prairie Points Diagrams,* fold each 3" square in quarters diagonally to make prairie points *(Diagrams A and B).*

Working from the front, arrange about 60 prairie points on each side of quilt, slipping folded edge into open edges to overlap *(Diagram C).* When satisfied with placement, stitch, then fold points to outside *(Diagram D).*

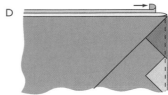

Blindstitch backing to points *(Diagram E).*

Border Triangle Template

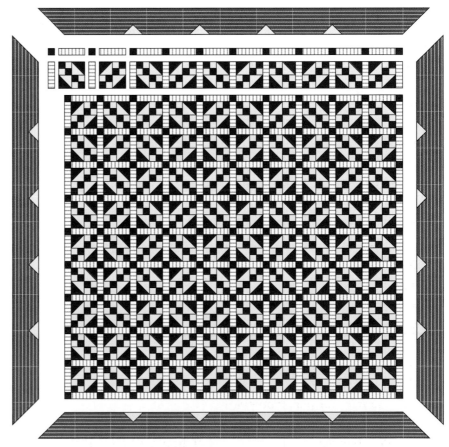

Quilt Top Assembly Diagram

Rosemary Zaugg
Weatherford, Texas

When Rosemary Zaugg was in high school, she made a list of things she wanted to do during her lifetime. "They included a college degree, to marry someone to share my quirky sense of humor, make a quilt, hold a grandchild, meet the Pope, etc." she says. "So my first year out of high school, I used cardboard templates and tediously cut out pieces for a star quilt in pink and white florals. At the time, I declared it to be my first and last project. It was not a great quilt, but my daughter has it now. And she calls it an antique quilt!"

Rosemary was a stay-at-home mom for several years. She then went to college and got her accounting degree in 1986 at age 41. Unfortunately, she had to quit

"Red to me is the color of life. My philosophy is to celebrate the gift of life in all that I do."

working in 1991, due to chronic hepatitis. The next year she received a liver transplant. "When I knew I could not go back to working long hours, I began looking at my friend's quilting magazine and decided to piece a quilt," she recalls. "It quickly became my hobby, my therapy, my passion, my love, and my legacy to our daughters. To make up for lost time, I have made 38 queen- or king-sized bed quilts; over 100 mini quilts, wall quilts, and table runners; 90 baby quilts; 10 patchwork jackets for me; and 2 jackets for my granddaughters."

Rosemary has served two years as treasurer of the 400-member Trinity Valley Quilters Guild. She was co-founder of the Quilter's Guild of Parker County, where she also served as treasurer. She is currently president of that group for the 2003–2004 year. She is also a member of the Appliqué Society and belongs to four smaller bees that meet monthly.

I Like Red
2000

Rosemary wanted to combine her favorite things in making this quilt: Log Cabin blocks, appliqué, paper piecing, and the color red. "Red to me is the color of life," she says. "My philosophy is to celebrate the gift of life in all that I do."

It has been more than 10 years since Rosemary's liver transplant, so she has added many

more things to her "to-do" list. "I have given back by donating eight quilts to various charities for raffle quilts," she says. "These 10 years have given me more time with my best friend—my husband of 36 years, the opportunity to see our two daughters marry and build stable marriages, hold four precious grandchildren, make many

new quilting friends, and see this quilt juried into the International Quilt Festival in Houston in 2002!"

The quilt also won Member's Choice 1st Place in the 2001 Trinity Valley Quilt Show, 2nd Place and People's Choice at the 2000 Senior Center Quilt Show, and 1st Place at the 2001 Weatherford Peach Festival.

I Like Red

Finished Size
Quilt: 87⅜" x 87⅜"
Blocks: 44 (9") Log Cabin
Blocks, 16 (9") Appliqué Blocks,
24 Border Blocks

Materials
3¼ yards white print for border
    and appliqué blocks
2½ yards total assorted white
    prints for blocks
6 yards total assorted red prints
    for blocks
1 yard red print for vine
1¼ yards red print for leaves and
    binding
1 fat quarter (18" x 22") red
    batik for berries
7⅞ yards fabric for backing
Queen-size batting

Cutting
Instructions are for rotary cutting
and quick piecing. Cut pieces in
order listed to make best use of
yardage. Patterns are on page 123.

From white print, cut:
- 2½ yards. Cut yardage into
  4 (6"-wide) lengthwise strips.
  Trim strips to make 2 (6" x
  76⅞") top and bottom borders
  and 2 (6" x 87⅞") side borders.
- From remainder, cut 9 (9½")
  squares for appliqué blocks.
- 2 (9½"-wide) strips. Cut strips
  into 7 (9½") squares for
  appliqué blocks. You will need
  16 squares total.

From assorted white prints, cut:
- 44 (1½") squares (#2).
- 44 (1½" x 2½") strips (#3).
- 44 (1½" x 3½") strips (#6).
- 44 (1½" x 4½") strips (#7).

*Professionally machine-quilted by Kathy Olson of
Treasured Threads in Granbury, Texas.*

- 44 (1½" x 5½") strips (#10).
- 44 (1½" x 6½") strips (#11).
- 44 (1½" x 7½") strips (#14).
- 44 (1½" x 8½") strips (#15).

From assorted red prints, cut:
- 68 (1½") squares (#1).
- 68 (1½" x 2½") strips (#4).
- 68 (1½" x 3½") strips (#5).
- 68 (1½" x 4½") strips (#8).
- 68 (1½" x 5½") strips (#9).
- 68 (1½" x 6½") strips (#12).
- 68 (1½" x 7½") strips (#13).
- 68 (1½" x 8½") strips (#16).
- 68 (1½" x 9½") strips (#17).
- 16 sets of 8 As.
- 16 Bs.

From red print for vine, cut:
- 450" of ¾"-wide bias. Fold and
  press in thirds to make ¼"-wide
  bias strip for main vine.
- 250" of 9/16"-wide bias. Fold and
  press in thirds to make 3/16"-
  wide bias strip for small stems.
  You will need 94 (2"-long)
  stems and 10 (3½"-long) stems.

From red print for leaves, cut:
- 100 leaves.
- 10 (2¼"-wide) strips for binding.

From red print for berries, cut:
- 104 berries.

Block Assembly
1. To make Log Cabin blocks,
choose 1 each of assorted red and
white block pieces #1–#17. Place #2
atop #1 and stitch. Open and finger-
press seam to red. Position #3 as
shown and stitch. Open and finger-
press away from #1/#2 unit.
Continue working around block,
adding logs until complete, as
shown in *Log Cabin Block Diagram*.
Make 44 Log Cabin blocks.

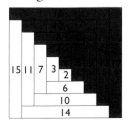

Log Cabin Block Diagram

2. To make Border Blocks, align end of #4 with end of #1 and stitch. Align #5 as shown in *Border Block Assembly Diagram* and add. Continue to alternate and add strips as shown to make 1 Border Block *(Border Block Diagram)*. Make 24 Border Blocks.

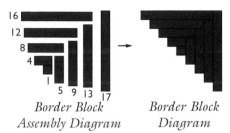

Border Block Assembly Diagram   *Border Block Diagram*

3. To make Appliqué Blocks, choose 1 B and 1 set of 8 As. Position on 1 appliqué background square as shown in *Appliqué Placement Diagram* and appliqué. Make 16 Appliqué Blocks.

Appliqué Placment Diagram

Quilt Assembly

1. Lay out blocks and border blocks as shown in *Quilt Top Assembly Diagram*. Join into diagonal rows; join rows to complete quilt center.

2. Add top and bottom borders, stitching across diagonal of border blocks. Trim excess from back.

3. Add side borders, aligning as above. Trim.

4. On each border, position main vine and small stems as shown in photo. When satisfied with placement, appliqué in position. Add leaves and berries.

Quilting and Finishing

1. Divide backing fabric into 3 (2⅝-yard) lengths. Cut 1 piece in half lengthwise. Sew 1 narrow panel between wide panel. Press seam allowances toward narrow panel. Remaining panel is extra and may be used to make a hanging sleeve. Seams will run horizontally.

2. Layer backing, batting, and quilt top; baste. Quilt as desired. Quilt shown is outline-quilted around appliqué in blocks and border, with backgrounds meander-quilted. Log Cabin blocks feature architectural motifs.

3. Join 2¼"-wide red print strips into 1 continuous piece for straight-grain French-fold binding. Add binding to quilt.

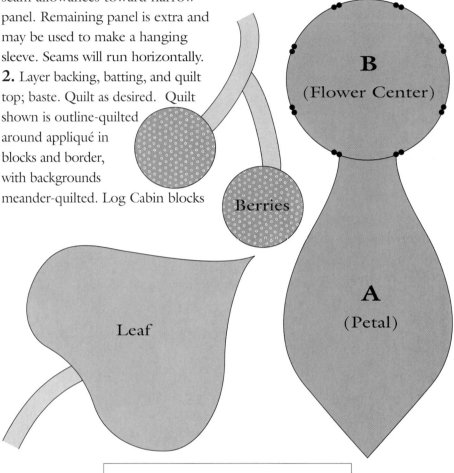

Quilt Top Assembly Diagram

Joanne Donahue and the Pony Express Quilters
Evansville, Indiana

*J*oanne Donahue has been quilting for more than 16 years. Her grandmother was an avid quilter, although she passed away before Joanne became interested in the art. Joanne recalls that her grandmother always had a quilt in the frame, which she inherited and now uses to quilt her own work.

"Quilting is my peace time," says Joanne. "I use it for quiet relaxation after work and as an outlet for creativity. My two daughters, Janelle and Caitlin, do not seem interested in the art form, but they do enjoy sleeping under my creations. I am thrilled each time I walk into a room and see one of my quilts displayed either on a bed or on a wall. The color, texture, and design of quilts lifts my spirits."

Joanne is a current member and former president of the Raintree Quilters

"Quilting is my peace time. I use it for quiet relaxation after work and as an outlet for creativity."

Guild of Evansville, Indiana. She also belongs to the Pony Express Quilters, a group of 12 friends who have met monthly for the last 10 years. It was this group that helped Joanne create *Spring Has Sprung*. Members of the bee include Liz Chandler, Cindy Garrett, Jan Clayton, Mary Anne Loehr, Michele Wisla, Amy Tank, Lynn Simmons, Betty Cummings, and Marcia Forston.

Spring Has Sprung
2001

Joanne's quilting bee, the Pony Express Quilters, have a yearly block exchange. Each member is required to make blocks for all the other members' quilts.

"I have always liked the Goose Tracks block," says Joanne, "so I asked each member to make two blocks in the blue and yellow fabrics supplied. The color scheme

was inspired by a fat quarter collection given to me by my friend, Liz Chandler. I enjoyed making the extra blocks needed and working in the coordinated scrap look."

Joanne decided to set the blocks on point with sashing, hoping to give the blocks a floating appearance.

"I spent two years intricately hand-quilting the piece," Joanne confesses. "I finished the quilt at the annual weekend retreat of the Pony Express Quilters at a local state park."

Spring Has Sprung was juried into the group quilt category at the 2002 American Quilter's Society show in Paducah, Kentucky.

Spring Has Sprung

Finished Size

Quilt: 92¼" x 108½"
Blocks: 50 (10") Goose Tracks
Blocks

Materials

35 fat quarters (18" x 22") yellow
  prints (use more for greater
  variety)
50 (3½" x 7") pieces medium blue
  prints (or 9 fat eighths)
25 fat eighths (9" x 22") dark blue
  prints
2 yards blue-and-yellow floral print
  for borders
1½ yards navy print for inner
  border and binding
8¼ yards for backing
King-size batting

Cutting

Instructions are for rotary cutting and quick piecing. Cut
pieces in order listed to make
best use of yardage.

From assorted yellows, cut:
- 50 sets of:
  - 4 (2½") B squares.
  - 4 (2½" x 4½") E rectangles.
  - 2 (3¼") squares. Cut
    squares in quarters diagonally
    to make 8 A triangles.
- 31 (2") squares for sashing
  squares.
- 80 (2" x 10½") sashing strips.
- 5 (17¾") squares. Cut squares
  in quarters diagonally to make
  20 side setting triangles. You
  will have 2 extra.
- 2 (8") squares. Cut squares in
  half diagonally to make 4 corner
  setting triangles.

*From assorted medium blue prints,
cut:*

- 50 sets of 2 (3⅜") squares. Cut
  squares in half diagonally to
  make 50 sets of 4 D triangles.

From assorted dark blue prints, cut:
- 50 sets of:
  - 2 (3¼") squares. Cut
    squares in quarters diagonally
    to make 8 A triangles.
  - 4 Cs.
  - 1 (2½") F square.

From yellow-and-blue print, cut:
- 12 (5½"-wide) strips. Join in
  groups of 3 to make 4 outer
  border strips.

From navy print, cut:
- 12 (2"-wide) strips. Join in
  groups of 3 to make 4 inner
  border strips.
- 11 (2¼"-wide) strips for binding.

Block Assembly

1. Choose 1 set each yellow, medium blue, and dark blue pieces.
2. Join 1 yellow and 1 dark blue
A triangles to make 1 triangle
unit. Make 8
triangle units,
placing colors
as shown in
*Quadrant
Assembly
Diagram.*

*Quadrant Assembly
Diagram*

3. Referring to *Quadrant Assembly
Diagram,* join 2 triangle units to 1
B square. Join 1 medium D to 1
dark C. Join as shown to make 1
quadrant. Make 4 quadrants.
4. Referring to *Block Assembly
Diagram,* lay out quadrants with
Es and F. Join into rows; join

126

rows to complete 1 Goose Tracks block *(Block Diagram)*. Make 50 Goose Tracks blocks.

Block Assembly Diagram

Block Diagram

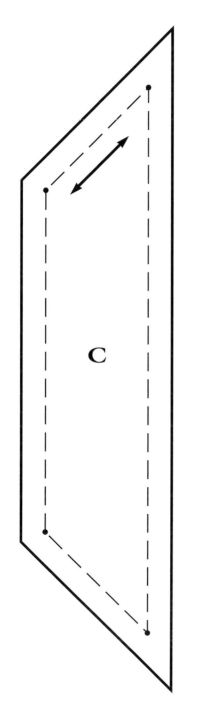

C

Quilt Assembly
Refer to *Quilt Top Assembly Diagram* throughout.

1. Lay out blocks with sashing, sashing squares, and setting triangles. Referring carefully to *Quilt Top Assembly Diagram*, join into diagonal rows. Join rows to complete quilt center.

2. Join 1 blue and 1 yellow strips to make 1 border strip. Make 4 border strips.

3. Center 1 border strip on each side of quilt and join. Miter corners.

Quilting and Finishing
1. Divide backing fabric into 3 (2¾-yard) lengths. Join along sides to make backing. Seams will run horizontally.

2. Layer backing, batting, and quilt top; baste. Quilt as desired. Quilt shown is outline-quilted in blocks and sashing with diamonds in E rectangles. Setting triangles feature Celtic knotwork, with twisted ribbons in inner border. Outer border has a braid pattern.

3. Join 2¼"-wide navy strips into 1 continuous piece for straight-grain French-fold binding. Add binding to quilt.

Quilt Top Assembly Diagram

Designer Gallery

We Fix Broken Hearts
Bright Hopes
Sitting Bull
Pharoah
Wedding Dreams

Ellen Guerrant
Charlotte, North Carolina

Photo by Matthew Guerrant

Although a stitcher since childhood, Ellen Guerrant did not begin quilting until 1980. At the time she was looking for a new diversion and decided to take a class. "The choices were tough—aerobics or quilting," Ellen recalls. "Quilting won, hands down! I mean, who wants to exercise when they can quilt?" Little did she know that decision would change her life.

Today, Ellen belongs to the Charlotte Quilter's Guild, where she has served two terms as president. She is also a member of Fiber Expressions, a regional group; the Art Quilt Network; the National Quilt Association; the International Quilt Association; the American Quilter's Society; the Professional Art Quilt Alliance-South; and the Studio Art Quilt Associates.

Ellen spends most of her time in the studio, but she also travels all over the country teaching for guilds and conferences. "Nothing gives me greater pleasure than getting someone excited about the infinite possibilities of quilting" she says.

"I can no longer just 'make a quilt.' It has to come from my heart. My quilts have become my voice."

Although she began as a traditionalist, Ellen's work now has a contemporary flair. Her quilts have won more than 50 ribbons, including a People's Choice and several Judge's Choice awards. Her quilts have appeared in 30 galleries throughout the United States and Canada and have been published.

"My work is now very personal," says Ellen. "I can no longer just 'make a quilt.' It has to come from my heart. My quilts have become my voice."

We Fix Broken Hearts
2002, 51" x 63"

When Ellen Guerrant's son Matthew turned 13, his doctors suddenly diagnosed him with end-stage heart failure. A heart transplant saved his life 47 days later.

"I could have said 'thank you' for the rest of my life, and it still would not have been enough," says Ellen. "Instead, I let *We Fix Broken Hearts* speak for me. Created to honor those who heal, the piece is a collage of hundreds of pieces of fabric stitched carefully back together by hand, just as human hearts are repaired. The hand images, traced from those of Matthew's cardiologists at The Sanger Clinic in Charlotte, North Carolina, not only hold the heart together physically, but also symbolize the spirit of many hands joining to heal the sick.

"Beading and hand painting on the top make the quilt glow, representing celebration of life."

Matthew is now 24 years old. A recent college graduate, he is a photographer living in High Point, North Carolina. He took the photo of his mother, above.

• *Juried into the 2003 World Quilt and Textile Show in Lansing, Michigan, and Manchester, New Hampshire*
• *Juried into Sacred Threads 2003 in Reynoldsburg, Ohio*
• *1st Place at the 2002 National Quilt Association Show*
• *Juried into a special exhibit at the 2002 International Quilt Association Show in Houston, Texas*
• *Exhibited at the Blue Pony Gallery in Charlotte, North Carolina*
• *Published in the January/February 2003 edition of* Quilter's Newsletter Magazine
• *Published in the Winter 2002 edition of* The Quilting Quarterly
• *Published in the Fall 2002* International Quilting Association Journal

• *2nd Place at the 2002 Quilter's Heritage Celebration in Lancaster, Pennsylvania*
• *2nd Place at the 2002 International Quilt Association Show in Houston, Texas*
• *Published on the November 2002 cover of* Quilter's Newsletter Magazine
Bright Hopes *is hand-appliquéd and machine-quilted.*

Karen Kay Buckley
Carlisle, Pennsylvania

Karen Kay Buckley began quilting in 1982, when the local high school offered a continuing education program in quilting. "Prior to that, I was getting into clothes sewing," says Karen. "But I quickly realized that with quilting, the finished product did not need to fit my body! I was immediately hooked."

Karen took many more classes. After about four years of working full-time and quilting in her spare time, her husband received a job offer in another area. To entice her to move into a metropolitan area, Joe suggested that Karen open her own quilt shop. So she did.

"The shop grew by leaps and bounds," says Karen. "The response to the shop was incredible. I started to develop my own classes and design my own projects. The classes were always full, and the students kept pushing me to develop more and more designs." After three years, Karen sold the shop and they moved again. This time, Karen had time to write.

"I enjoy every aspect of making a quilt, from drawing my designs on paper, to touching my fabric when selecting the colors for each project, to the actual sewing."

"I completed my first book, and it was published by the American Quilter's Society," Karen says. "I have since published four more books with them. I have worked with some other publishers on portions of books and have written articles for magazines." More recently, Karen has designed and published her own line of patterns.

"I love to quilt. It is my passion," Karen confesses. "I enjoy every aspect of making a quilt, from drawing my designs on paper, to touching my fabric when selecting the colors for each project, to the actual sewing. And one of the most gratifying things is seeing the finished quilt."

Bright Hopes
2002, 88" x 88"

A damask design inspired Karen Kay Buckley to make this quilt. "I have fallen in love with medallion-style quilts," she says.

"I am drawn to the symmetry and balance. I was finishing the design drawings for this quilt around September 11, 2001," she recalls.

"As I began selecting colors for the quilt, they kept getting brighter. I was hoping for a brighter future for us all."

Sharon Schamber
Jensen, Utah

Sharon Schamber, a member of the Southern California Quilt Guild, began quilting around 1998. "I am severely dyslexic, so I found it much easier to do all my own design work rather than to follow other's patterns," she says.

She entered her first competition in 1999. Her hand-pieced and hand-quilted *Victorian Flame* won Best of Show in the Jinny Beyer Borders on Brilliance competition in Houston, Texas. "It was then I decided to continue to compete," Sharon recalls. "I have now branched into hand painting, more machine quilting, and doing free-motion quilting on unmarked quilts."

Sharon spent 30 years in bridal and pageant gown design in Phoenix, Arizona. "After retiring from that business, I decided I wanted to quilt full-time. This has led to numerous competitions, and now, more and more of my time is spent teaching. I also design patterns, which are marketed with two free-motion pattern books through Jukebox Quilts."

> *"I am severely dyslexic, so I found it much easier to do all my own design work rather than to follow other's patterns."*

Although this new business takes a great deal of Sharon's time, she still continues to showcase her one-of-a-kind art quilts in major quilt shows throughout the country. Crowds gathered around her *Sitting Bull* quilt at the 2002 International Quilt Festival in Houston, Texas. One spectator commented, "His eyes seem to follow you wherever you move." To create this kind of reality in fabric is a rare gift.

Sitting Bull
2002, 90" x 93"

"I have always wanted to do some Native American work," says Sharon Schamber. "This subject was one of the most highly respected of the Lakota, and a photo was available for me to work from. It required much research to make sure every symbol and color was correct. I make all my own designs, and this is an original one-of-a-kind work. It is meant to exemplify the beauty and simplicity of Native American art.

"Sitting Bull's portrait is surrounded with authentic Lakota symbols, including the Ghost Dance Shirt in the lower left corner, the eagle in the upper right corner, the buffalo skull in the upper left corner, and the war shield in the lower right corner.

"Sitting Bull was murdered while being arrested by police in late 1890. It was feared by General N.A. Miles that he would lead a Ghost Dance and create another uprising."

- *Honorable Mention and a Faculty Choice Award from Bana Robinson at the 2002 Quilt the Quilt Show in Duluth, Minnesota. The show was sponsored by American Professional Quilting Systems.*
- *Honorable Mention at the 2002 International Quilt Festival in Houston, Texas*
- *Outstanding Large Quilt in the 2003 Road to California Show in Ontario, Canada*

- *Best of Show at the 2002 Quilter's Heritage Celebration in Lancaster, Pennsylvania*
- *1st Place in Traditional Quilts at the 2002 Mid-Atlantic Quilt Festival in Williamsburg, Virginia*
- *Best of Show at the Association of Pacific Northwest Quilters QuiltFest*
- *Master Award for Innovative Artistry at the 2002 International Quilt Festival in Houston, Texas*
- *Published in the October 2002 edition of* Quilter's Newsletter Magazine
- *Published in the October 30, 2002 edition of the* Houston Chronicle
- *Appeared on the PBS documentary, "QuiltFest: For the Love of Fabric."*

Sandra Frieze Leichner
Albany, Oregon

*S*andra Frieze Leichner began quilting in 1999, after her third child was born. "I had stopped painting with the birth of my first child and was anxious to pick up my brushes again," she recalls. "I quickly realized that with three small children, painting was no longer an option for me. My mother had been quilting, and I decided to make a quilt for my youngest child. I wasn't aware that you were supposed to start with the easy stuff. I came up with my own intricate appliqué design and taught myself to hand appliqué through many trials and errors. I never finished that baby quilt, but my love for appliqué was born. I was finally able to return to painting again, only now, my medium is fiber."

"I was finally able to return to painting again, only now, my medium is fiber."

A member of the International Quilt Association, the Pacific Northwest Quilt Association, and the American Quilter's Society, Sandra admits that quilting is an important part of her life. "I spend a good portion of my day working on new ideas and projects. Even though I have a traditional style, I am careful to leave my mind open to learning new techniques during the creative process so my designs can evolve into the finished quilt I have envisioned. I have found that most of what we think is new today has actually been done at least 100 years ago by a creative quilter. I am very fortunate to be able to combine my passions for design, history, and fiber to create quilted art."

Pharaoh
2001, 76" x 82"

Her parents' recent trip to Egypt inspired Sandra to design *Pharaoh*. "I wanted to make a quilt that depicted the original colors and artistry of the painted tombs," she says.

Although Sandra had always been fascinated with ancient Egyptian art, her parents' recent trip to Egypt set the quilt into motion. Sandra spent two months researching Egypt before sketching her design.

"The design incorporates the symbolism and artistic style of the ancient Egyptians," she says. "The quilt also served unexpectedly as a teaching aid for my oldest son after he had been frightened by a mummy nightmare. I used the quilt and my research books to teach my son about ancient Egypt and to dispel the myths regarding mummies. My son has developed an interest in Egyptology and would like to visit the pyramids."

Detail

Maria Elkins
Dayton, Ohio

*M*aria Elkins fell in love with fabric and thread at an early age, when her mother let her play with her bag of fabric scraps. Her mother taught her embroidery at age five, and at nine, she taught her to use the sewing machine and read a pattern. By junior high, Maria was sewing most of her own clothes. Her father was so proud of her, he bought her a sewing machine when she turned 14.

"While I would like for quilting to play a central role in my life, for now I must squeeze it in between my full-time job, my husband, my two teenage daughters, and all the extra activities that go along with a busy family," says Maria. "In fall 2002, I also started going back to college to finish the Bachelor of Fine Arts degree that I started years ago, before I got married and had kids."

Maria admits she was obsessed while making *Wedding Dreams*. "I worked on it every waking moment for ten months," she recalls. "I woke up early and sewed before I went to work. I stayed up late to sew. I even took vacation days and sewed from before dawn until after my usual bed-time. Still, I missed the deadline for the quilt guild

> *"While I would like for quilting to play a central role in my life, for now I must squeeze it in...."*

challenge! I ended up entering the top only, just to show what I had done."

"Since making *Wedding Dreams*, I have decided to concentrate on small quilts until I have more time to devote to quilting," Maria says. "My goal is to make two or three smaller wall hangings each year, using techniques that will help me finish the quilt in less time while maintaining high quality."

Wedding Dreams
2001, 68" x 68"

Maria Elkins designed this quilt in response to a challenge sponsored by the Miami Valley Quilter's Guild of Dayton, Ohio. "The theme of the challenge was 'Visions of Tomorrow,' and before I was even home from the guild meeting, I could already see the completed quilt in my mind," says Maria.

"My self-imposed challenge was to achieve a feeling of movement and the suggestion of transparency in the veil. The quilt captures the image of a young girl as she dances and twirls and day-dreams about what she will look like on her wedding day. Since the bride is the grown-up version of the girl, I echoed the dreamy expression on her face and repeated the same body and clothing positions."

The quilt is completely machine-pieced (not appliquéd), except for the faces and the bride's bouquet, which are hand appliquéd. The quilt is machine-quilted with rayon, metallic, and kaleidoscope threads.

- Juried into the 2003 Quilt Odyssey in Gettysburg, Pennsylvania
- 1st Place, Master Division Art Quilt at the 2003 Dallas Quilt Celebration in Dallas, Texas
- 2nd Place, Bed Mixed Media at the 2003 Sew Near to My Heart Show in Cincinnati, Ohio
- Honorable Mention, Innovative Wall Mixed Techniques at the 2003 Road to California Quilters Conference and Showcase in Ontario, California
- Best Machine Workmanship and Honorable Mention for Innovative Category at the 2002 Pennsylvania National Quilt Extravaganza VIII in New Hope, Pennsylvania
- Viewer's Choice and 1st Place Large Wall Quilts, Pieced, Machine-Quilted at the 2002 National Quilting Association Annual Show in Charlotte, North Carolina
- Best of Show, 1st Place Innovative Piecing, and Channel 2 Media Award at the 2002 Miami Valley Quilter's Guild Show
- Juried into 2002 American Quilters Society Show in Paducah, Kentucky
- 2nd Place Fabric Art, Amateur at the 2002 Indiana Heritage Quilt Show in Bloomington, Indiana
- Juried into the 2001 International Quilt Association Show in Houston, Texas
- Workmanship Award and Viewer's Choice Award at the 2001 Quilt America! Show in Indianapolis, Indiana

QUILT SMART WORKSHOP
A Guide to Quiltmaking

Preparing Fabric

Before cutting any pieces, be sure to wash and dry your fabric to preshrink it. All-cotton fabrics may need pressing before cutting. Trim selvages from the fabric before you cut pieces.

Making Templates

Before you can make one of the quilts in this book, you must make templates from the printed patterns given. (Not all pieces require patterns—some pieces are meant to be cut with a rotary cutter and ruler.) Quilters have used many materials to make templates, including cardboard and sandpaper. Transparent template plastic, available at craft supply and quilt shops, is durable, see-through, and easy to use.

To make a plastic template, place the plastic sheet on the printed page and use a laundry marker or permanent fine-tip marking pen to trace each pattern. For machine piecing, trace on the outside solid (cutting) line. For hand piecing, trace on the inside broken (stitching) line. Cut out the template on the traced line. Label each template with the pattern name, letter, grain line arrow, and match points (corner dots).

Marking and Cutting Fabric for Piecing

Place the template facedown on the wrong side of the fabric and mark around it with a sharp pencil.

If you will be piecing by machine, the pencil lines represent cutting lines. Cut on each marked line.

For hand piecing, the pencil lines are seam lines. Leave at least ¾" between marked lines for seam allowances. Add ¼" seam allowance around each piece as you cut. Mark match points (corner dots) on each piece.

You can do without templates if you use a rotary cutter and ruler to cut straight strips and geometric shapes such as squares and triangles. Rotary cutting

is always paired with machine piecing, and pieces are cut with seam allowances included.

Hand Piecing

To hand piece, place two fabric pieces together with right sides facing. Insert a pin in each match point of the top piece. Stick the pin through both pieces and check to be sure that it pierces the match point on the bottom piece

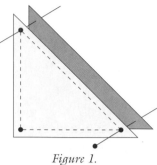

*Figure 1.
Aligning Match Points*

(*Figure 1*). Adjust the pieces as necessary to align the match points. (The raw edges of the two pieces may not align exactly.) Pin the pieces securely together.

Sew with a running stitch of 8 to 10 stitches per inch. Sew from match point to match point, checking the stitching as you go to be sure you are sewing in the seam line of both pieces.

To make sharp corners, begin and end the stitching exactly at the match point; do not stitch into the seam allowances. When joining units where several seams come together, do not sew over seam allowances; sew through them at the point where all seam lines meet (*Figure 2*).

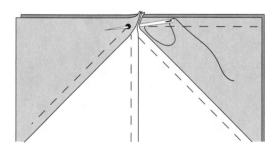

Figure 2. Joining Units

Always press both seam allowances to one side. Pressing the seam open, as in dress-making, can leave gaps between stitches through which the batting may beard. Press seam allowances toward the darker fabric

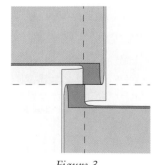

*Figure 3.
Pressing Intersecting Seams*

whenever you can, but it is sometimes more important to reduce bulk by avoiding overlapping seam allowances. When four or more seams meet at one point, such as at the corner of a block, press all the seams in a "swirl" in the same direction to reduce bulk (*Figure 3*).

Machine Piecing

To machine piece, place two fabric pieces together with right sides facing. Align match points as described under "Hand Piecing" and pin the pieces together securely.

Set the stitch length at 12 to 15 stitches per inch. At this setting, you do not need to backstitch to lock seam beginnings and ends. Use a presser foot that gives a perfect ¼" seam allowance, or measure ¼" from the needle and mark that point on the presser foot with nail polish or masking tape.

Chain piecing, stitching edge to edge, saves time when sewing similar sets of pieces (*Figure 4*). Join the

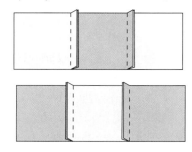

Figure 4. Chain Piecing

first two pieces as usual. At the end of the seam, do not backstitch, cut the thread, or lift the presser foot. Instead, sew a few stitches off the fabric. Place the next two pieces and continue stitching. Keep sewing until all the sets are joined. Then cut the sets apart.

Press seam allowances toward the darker fabric whenever possible. When you join blocks or rows, press the seam allowances of the top row in one direction and the seam allowances of the bottom row in the opposite direction to help ensure that the seams will lie flat (*Figure 5*).

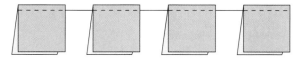

*Figure 5.
Pressing Seams for Machine Piecing*

Hand Appliqué

Hand appliqué is the best way to achieve the look of traditional appliqué. But using freezer paper, which

is sold in grocery stores, saves time because it eliminates the need for hand basting seam allowances.

Make templates without seam allowances. Trace the template onto the *dull* side of the freezer paper; cut the paper on the marked line. Make a freezer-paper shape for each piece to be appliquéd.

Pin the freezer-paper shape, *shiny side up*, to the *wrong side* of the fabric. Following the paper shape and adding a scant ¼" seam allowance, cut out the fabric piece. Do not remove the pins. Use the tip of a hot, dry iron to press the seam allowance to the shiny side of the freezer paper. Be careful not to touch the shiny side of the freezer paper with the iron. Remove the pins.

Pin the appliqué shape in place on the background fabric. Use one strand of sewing thread in a color to match the appliqué shape. Using a very small slipstitch (*Figure 6*) or blindstitch (*Figure 7*), appliqué the shape to the background fabric.

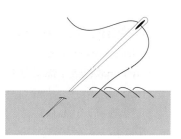

Figure 6. Slipstitch

When your stitching is complete, cut away the background fabric behind the appliqué, leaving ¼" seam allowance. Separate the freezer paper from the

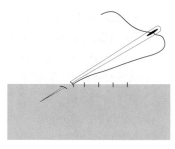

Figure 7. Blindstitch

fabric with your fingernail and pull gently to remove it.

Mitering Borders

Mitered borders take a little extra care to stitch but offer a nice finish when square border corners just won't do.

First, measure the length of the quilt through the middle of the quilt top. Cut two border strips to fit this length, plus the width of the border plus 2". Centering the measurement on the strip, place pins on the edge of each strip at the center and each end of the measurement. Match the pins on each border strip to the corners of a long side of the quilt. Starting and stopping ¼" from each corner of the quilt, sew the borders to the quilt, easing the quilt to fit between the pins (*Figure 8*). Press seam allowances toward border strip.

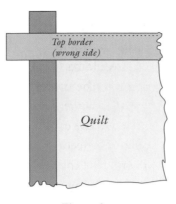

Figure 8

Measure the quilt width through the middle and cut two border strips to fit, adding the border width plus 2". Join these borders to opposite ends of the quilt in the same manner.

Fold one border corner over the adjacent corner (*Figure 9*) and press. On the wrong side, stitch in the creased fold to stitch a mitered seam (*Figure 10*). Press; then check to make sure the corner lies flat on the quilt top. Trim seam allowances.

Fold end of top border under to align with end of side border.

Quilt

Figure 9

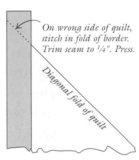

On wrong side of quilt, stitch in fold of border. Trim seam to ¼". Press.

Diagonal fold of quilt

Figure 10

Marking Your Quilt Top

When the quilt top is complete, press it thoroughly before marking it with quilting designs. The most popular methods for marking use stencils or templates. Both can be purchased, or you can make your own. You can also use a yardstick to mark straight lines or grids.

Use a silver quilter's pencil for marking light to medium fabrics and a white chalk pencil on dark fabrics. Lightly mark the quilt top with your chosen quilting designs.

Making a Backing

The instructions in *Great American Quilts* give backing yardage based on 45"-wide fabric unless a 90"-wide or 108"-wide backing is more practical. (These fabrics are sold at fabric and quilt shops.) Pieced or not, the quilt backing should be at least 3" larger on all sides than the quilt top.

Backing fabric should be of a type and color that is compatible with the quilt top. Percale sheets are not recommended, because they are tightly woven and difficult to hand-quilt through.

A pieced backing for a bed quilt should have three panels. The three-panel backing is recommended because it tends to wear better and lie flatter than the two-panel type, the center seam of which often makes a ridge down the center of the quilt. Begin by cutting the fabric in half widthwise (*Figure 11*).

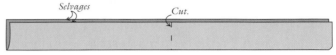

Selvages   Cut.

Figure 11

Open the two lengths and stack them, with right sides facing and selvages aligned. Stitch along both selvage edges to create a tube of fabric (*Figure 12*). Cut down the center of the top layer of fabric *only* and open the fabric flat (*Figure 13*). Press seam allowances toward center panel.

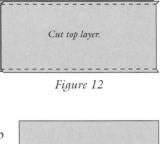

Cut top layer.

Figure 12

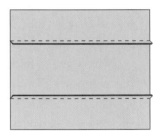

Figure 13

Layering and Basting

Prepare a working surface to spread out the quilt. Place the backing on the surface, right side down. Unfold the batting and place it on top of the backing. Smooth any wrinkles or lumps in the batting. Lay the quilt top right side up on top of the batting and backing. Make sure backing and quilt top are parallel.

Use a darning needle for basting, with a long strand of sewing thread. Begin in the center of your quilt and baste out toward the edges. The stitches should cover enough of the quilt to keep the layers from shifting during quilting. Inadequate basting can result in puckers and folds on the back and front of the quilt during quilting.

Hand Quilting

Hand quilting can be done with the quilt in a hoop or in a floor frame. It is best to start in the middle of your quilt and quilt out toward the edges.

Most quilters use a thin, short needle called a "between." Betweens are available in sizes 7 to 12, with 7 being the longest and 12 the shortest. If you are a beginning quilter, try a size 7 or 8. Because betweens are so much shorter than other needles, they may feel awkward at first. As your skill increases, try using a smaller needle to help you make smaller stitches.

Quilting thread, heavier and stronger than sewing thread, is available in a wide variety of colors. If color matching is critical and you can't find the color you need, you can substitute cotton sewing thread if you coat it with beeswax before quilting to prevent it from tangling.

Thread your needle with a 20" length and make a small knot at one end. Insert the needle into the quilt top approximately ½" from the point where you want to begin quilting. Do not take the needle through all three layers, but stop it in the batting and bring it up through the quilt top again at your starting point. Tug gently on the thread to pop the knot through the quilt top into the batting. This anchors the thread without an unsightly knot showing on the back.

With your non-sewing hand underneath the quilt, insert the needle with the point straight down in the quilt about ¹⁄₁₆" from the starting point. With your underneath finger, feel for the point as the needle comes through the backing (*Figure 14*).

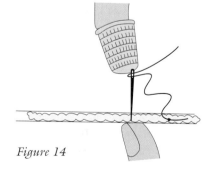

Figure 14

Place the thumb of your sewing hand approximately ½" ahead of the needle. When you feel the needle touch your underneath finger, push the fabric up from below as you rock the needle down to a nearly horizontal position. Using the thumb of your sewing hand in conjunction with the underneath hand, pinch a little hill in the fabric and push the tip of the needle back through the quilt top (*Figure 15*).

Figure 15

Now either push the needle all the way through to complete one stitch or rock the needle again to an upright position on its point to take another stitch. Take no more than a quarter-needleful of stitches before pulling the needle through.

When you have 6" of thread remaining, you must end the old thread securely and invisibly. Carefully tie a knot in the thread, flat against the surface of the fabric. Pop the knot through the top as you did when beginning the line of quilting. Clip the thread, rethread your needle, and continue quilting.

Machine Quilting

Machine quilting is as old as the sewing machine itself; but until recently, it was thought inferior to hand quilting. Fine machine quilting is an exclusive category, but it requires a different set of skills from hand quilting.

Machine quilting can be done on your sewing machine using a straight stitch and a special presser foot. A walking foot or even-feed foot is recommended for straight-line quilting to help the top fabric move through the machine at the same rate that the feed dogs move the bottom fabric.

Regular sewing thread or nylon thread can be used for machine quilting. With the quilt top facing you, roll the long edges of the basted quilt toward the center, leaving a 12"-wide area unrolled in the center. Secure the roll with bicycle clips, metal bands that are available at quilt shops. Begin at one unrolled end and fold the quilt over and over until only a small area is showing. This will be the area where you will begin to quilt.

Place the folded portion of the quilt in your lap. Start quilting in the center and work to the right, unfolding and unrolling the quilt as you go. Remove the quilt from the machine, turn it, and reinsert it in the machine to stitch the left side. A table placed behind your sewing machine will help support the quilt as it is stitched.

   Curves and circles are most easily made by free-motion machine quilting. Using a darning foot and with the feed dogs down, move the quilt under the needle with your fingertips. Place your hands on the fabric on each side of the foot and run the machine at a steady, medium speed. The length of the stitches is determined by the rate of speed at which you move fabric through the machine. Do not rotate the quilt; rather, move it from side to side as needed. Always stop with the needle down to keep the quilt from shifting.

Making Binding

A continuous bias or straight-grain strip is used to bind quilt edges. Bias binding is especially recommended for quilts with curved edges. Follow these steps to make a continuous bias strip:

1. Start with a square of fabric. Multiply the number of binding inches needed by the cut width of the binding strip (usually 2½"). Use a calculator to find the square root of that number. That's the size of the fabric square needed to make your binding.

2. Cut the square in half diagonally.

3. With right sides facing, join triangles to form a sawtooth as shown *(Figure 16)*.

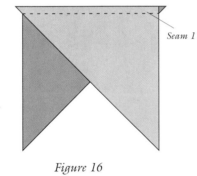

Figure 16

4. Press seam open. Mark off parallel lines the desired width of the binding as shown *(Figure 17)*.

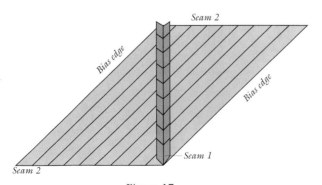

Figure 17

5. With right sides facing, align raw edges marked Seam 2. Offset edges by one strip width, so one side is higher than the other *(Figure 18)*. Stitch Seam 2. Press seam open.

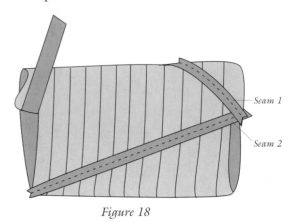

Figure 18

6. Cut the binding in a continuous strip, starting with the protruding point and following the marked lines around the tube.

7. Press the binding strip in half lengthwise, with wrong sides facing.

Attaching Binding

To prepare your quilt for binding, baste the layers together ¼" from the edge of the quilt. Trim the backing and batting even with the edge of the quilt top. Beginning at the midpoint of one side of the quilt, pin the binding to the top, with right sides facing and raw edges aligned.

   Machine-stitch the binding along one edge of the quilt, sewing through all layers. Backstitch at the beginning of the seam to lock the stitching.

   Stitch until you reach the seam line at the corner, and backstitch. Lift the presser foot and turn the quilt to align the foot with the next edge. Miter fabric at corner. Continue sewing around all four sides. Join the beginning and end of the binding strip by machine.

   Turn the binding over the edge and blindstitch it in place on the backing. At each corner, fold the excess binding neatly to make a mitered corner and blindstitch it in place.